Delight Your
CUSTOMERS

Delight Your
CUSTOMERS

7

SIMPLE WAYS TO RAISE YOUR CUSTOMER SERVICE
from
ORDINARY TO EXTRAORDINARY

Steve Curtin

AMACOM

AMERICAN MANAGEMENT ASSOCIATION

New York • Atlanta • Brussels • Chicago • Mexico City • San Francisco
Shanghai • Tokyo • Toronto • Washington, D.C.

Bulk discounts available. For details visit: www.amacombooks.org/go/specialsales
Or contact special sales: Phone: 800-250-5308 E-mail: specialsls@amanet.org
View all the AMACOM titles at: www.amacombooks.org
American Management Association: www.amanet.org

This publication is designed to provide accurate and authoritative information in regard to the subject matter covered. It is sold with the understanding that the publisher is not engaged in rendering legal, accounting, or other professional service. If legal advice or other expert assistance is required, the services of a competent professional person should be sought.

LIBRARY OF CONGRESS CATALOGING-IN-PUBLICATION DATA
Curtin, Steve.
Delight your customers : 7 simple ways to raise your customer service
from ordinary to extraordinary / Steve Curtin.—1 Edition.
pages cm
Includes index.
ISBN 978-0-8144-3280-8—ISBN 0-8144-3280-8 1. Consumer satisfaction.
2. Product management. 3. Organizational change. I. Title.
HF5415.335.C867 2013
658.8'12—dc23   2013004338

About AMA

American Management Association (www.amanet.org) is a world leader in talent development, advancing the skills of individuals to drive business success. Our mission is to support the goals of individuals and organizations through a complete range of products and services, including classroom and virtual seminars, webcasts, webinars, podcasts, conferences, corporate and government solutions, business books, and research. AMA's approach to improving performance combines experiential learning—learning through doing—with opportunities for ongoing professional growth at every step of one's career journey.

Printing number

10 9 8 7 6 5 4 3

Contents

PART TWO: SEVEN SIMPLE WAYS TO
RAISE CUSTOMER SERVICE

Acknowledgments

On December 15, 2011, I received a four-sentence email from literary agent Michael Snell. Thus began an 18-month odyssey culminating with this book.

Like most ventures into the unknown, there was a cast of characters that provided the guidance and expertise needed to reach the goal. Without the counsel of Michael Snell during multiple iterations of the book proposal over the course of several months, *Delight Your Customers* would have remained the book inside me waiting to get out.

After Michael found a home for the project at AMACOM Books, I worked with senior editor Bob Nirkind. Bob provided direction, structuring a lot of meandering ideas into a clear roadmap showing readers how to better serve customers. As we neared the journey's end, we received expert help from associate editor Jim Bessent and illustrator Aaron McKissen.

As I reflect on the book's customer service message, I'd like to thank the many colleagues during my 20-year career at Marriott International who defined and modeled the difference between ordinary and extraordinary, including: Mark Conklin, Ted Scholz, Susan Belleville, Jeff Gray, Jean Cohen, Ray Falcone, Victor Aragona, Eileen James, Nancy Curtin Morris, Curt Newport, David Toomey, Brian O'Neill, and the late John Barclay.

Of course, none of this would have been possible without support at home. I'm grateful to our intrepid nanny and budding novelist, Amberle, for lending her copyediting talents along the way. And to the love of my life, Julie, and our four amazing children, thank you for your encouragement throughout this adventure.

Delight Your
CUSTOMERS

Introduction

Years ago, I worked in New York City with an English woman named Karen who had a unique work history. During graduate school in England, she had worked on an assembly line in a factory that manufactured dolls.

Karen's job role was to attach doll heads to each of the torsos as they passed by on a long conveyer belt. As she described it, as the torso approached, she would lift a doll head from a large bin, pop the head on the torso, and twist it firmly until it locked into place. One by one, Karen would lift, pop, and twist the dolls' heads into place—each one like the last one—until her quota was met or her shift ended. The next day, she would return and repeat the process over and over again: lift, pop, twist ... lift, pop, twist ... until the end of another workday. I can still hear Karen describing her job duties in her refined British accent: "Leeft, paup, tweest ... Leeft, paup, tweest ... Leeft, paup, tweest ..."

To this day, whenever I observe an employee who is simply going through the motions, I'm reminded of Karen's job at the factory. I refer to this demeanor as a *factory mentality*. Perhaps you too have observed this outward behavior by service industry employees. It's easy to spot, characterized by indifference and a transactional approach to serving customers.

Expressionless, robotic behavior devoid of any personality may be permissible in a factory or warehouse environment where there are no signs of real, live, paying customers (as long as certain production quotas and delivery schedules are met). However, in a customer service job role, employee behavior must be different.

This is not a book about how to "WOW!" customers by continually surpassing their expectations and exceeding their needs—which is unsustainable. Most people don't want "outrageous" or "over-the-top" customer service at every turn. In everyday service situations, most customers simply want to be acknowledged and appreciated.

Delight Your Customers is about doing the little things that convey to customers that they matter and that their business is valued. It's about breaking with routine by consistently providing the "little extras" that leave lasting positive impressions on customers. After all, the difference between ordinary and extraordinary is that little "extra."

Part I sets the stage for delighting customers by identifying the two dimensions of every employee's job role and identifying three truths of exceptional customer service. Whether you are new to the service industry or a seasoned veteran, this section will expand your definition of employees' roles and is likely to influence the way you manage service providers.

Part II introduces seven concrete behaviors that will enable you to immediately improve the quality of customer service you provide or influence. These seven simple ways to raise customer service from ordinary to extraordinary are natural and intuitive. Rather than offering scripts or a prescriptive acronym that requires employees to be someone they're not, these behaviors encourage employees to be themselves at their best!

Part III provides fresh thinking about incorporating your organization's highest priority into existing employee functions so that exceptional customer service, however it is defined by your particular organization, occurs consistently rather than being left to chance.

Throughout the book, you will see references to customers, clients, guests, shoppers, passengers, patients, members, and more. The lessons in this book will apply, regardless of how you refer to your customers, even if your "customer" is an employee, owner, vendor, or other stakeholder. In fact, I'd go so far as to say that these lessons also apply to the "customers" you serve in your personal life, whether that means a spouse, children, friends, neighbors—even complete strangers.

Each chapter concludes with a bulleted summary of key insights to assist you in raising customer service from ordinary to extraordinary, followed by a brief application exercise in which you immediately record top-of-mind ideas about applying lessons from the chapter in your world of work.

It's no secret that the customer service quality most of us experience in our daily lives tends to be pretty mediocre. (And sometimes that assessment is being generous.) It's my aspiration to contribute to the conversation about raising customer service quality—and this book is a start. To continue the conversation, I invite you to visit my blog at http://www.stevecurtin.com/blog/ or email me: steve@stevecurtin.com

Yours in service,

Steve Curtin
Denver, Colorado
November 1, 2012

Part One

FUNCTION VS. ESSENCE

1

Three Truths of Exceptional Customer Service

If you want to find out just how bad customer service is, go buy something. It hardly even matters where you go, whom you call, or which website you visit. Sure, there are exceptions—those fabled companies that come to mind when one thinks about legendary customer service, like Zappos, Disney, L.L. Bean, Nordstrom, and Ritz-Carlton. But even then, the quality of your service experience hinges on the one-on-one interaction you have with a service provider, despite the company's acclaimed service culture.

But if you are not dealing with an exceptional company or an especially customer-focused service provider, chances are you are dealing with an average company or an indifferent employee in terms of customer service.

In my customer service seminars, I distinguish between the two aspects of every employee's job role: *job function*, the duties or tasks associated with the employee's job roles, and *job essence*, the employee's highest priority at work. Recognizing the difference between these two aspects is central to understanding why customer service quality is so predictably poor. In my seminars, I also share three truths that are common to all exceptional customer service experiences:

1. It reflects the essence—the most critical aspect, the highest priority—of every service industry employee's job role.
2. It is always voluntary. An employee *chooses* to deliver exceptional customer service.
3. In most cases, it costs no more to deliver than poor customer service. In other words, it's free.

Awareness is key. People don't know what they don't know.

The first thing to do to increase awareness and improve the quality of customer service delivery in any business is to ask employees this question: "Would you describe for me, from your perspective, what you do—what your job entails?"

When I pose this question to employees I encounter in hotels, shopping centers, supermarkets, or airports, the responses I receive almost always apply exclusively to their job functions.

Here's how my latest conversation with a supermarket employee went:

ME: "Pardon me. Do you mind if I ask what you do—what your job entails?"

EMPLOYEE: "Are you from corporate headquarters or something?"

ME: "No. I'm just interested in what you do."

EMPLOYEE: "Well, my job is to sack groceries, but when we're not busy, I bring in shopping carts from the lot and sweep the store. Sometimes I have to check prices or clean up spills. That's about it."

Every action mentioned has to do with job function. Rarely do employees reference actions or behaviors pertaining to job essence, which, ironically, should be their highest priority at work.

This brings us to the first truth of exceptional customer service.

Exceptional Customer Service Reflects the Essence of Every Service Industry Employee's Job Role

While employees consistently execute job function, they inconsistently demonstrate job essence. That's a problem, because job essence reflects an employee's highest priority at work. For employees at most service-oriented companies, this priority is, by his or her actions, to create a *promoter*. A promoter, according to the consulting firm Bain & Company, is a customer who is less price-sensitive, has higher repurchase rates, and is responsible for 80 to 90 percent of the positive word-of-mouth about a company or brand.

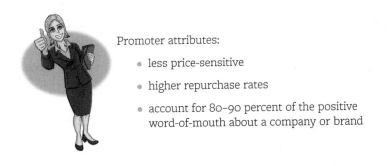

Promoter attributes:

- less price-sensitive

- higher repurchase rates

- account for 80–90 percent of the positive word-of-mouth about a company or brand

The challenge for employers is that, oftentimes, employees think that the functions and essence of their job roles are one and the same. When this happens, employees become transactional and process-focused, treating each customer like the last customer. A factory mentality ensues. In the short term, this practice may be highly efficient (employees process more customers more quickly), but in the long term, it is ineffective. It does not fulfill the organization's highest priority: to create promoters.

Consider your own organization. Do employees really know the difference between their job functions and the essence of their job? If you're not sure, just ask them. My hunch is that you will be met with blank stares. This then becomes an opportunity for you to have a meaningful conversation with your employees about the difference between

Job Function
The duiities or tasks associated
with a job role

Job Essence
Employees' highest priority at
work: to create a promoter

the tasks they are responsible for executing and your organization's highest priority.

Job function includes employees' job knowledge (what they do) and job skills (how they do it). Most employees are aware of their responsibility to execute job function and are proficient in this aspect of their work. And managers can recite job functions for most job roles in their sleep.

Consider the supermarket employee discussed above, and his list of what his job entails:

- Sack groceries (job function)
- Bring in shopping carts (job function)
- Sweep the store (job function)
- Check prices (job function)
- Clean up spills (job function)

Note that these are all job functions, the duties or tasks associated with his job role, and that there is no mention of any attention to job essence.

Job essence reflects employees' motivation (why they do it). Employees are typically less clear about this dimension of their job roles, mainly because they are focused on job function. What motivates employees individually—their unique purpose or vision for their lives—is beyond the scope of this book (although the most effective leaders do engage their employees to glean insight into what motivates each of them *as individuals*). For our purposes, we are simply considering the organization's priorities: Why does the organization exist? What is its purpose? And what role does the employee play in contributing to this purpose?

For example, Zappos has aligned the entire organization around one mission: to provide the best customer service possible. Everything its employees do—from receiving a merchandise order at its contact center, through order fulfillment, to (when required) product returns—is geared toward providing the best customer service possible. This is the essence of every Zappos employee's job role, and it informs every decision employees make. This is especially critical when employees are faced with a decision of whether or not to express genuine interest in a caller or to pleasantly surprise a customer by expediting the shipping of her order.

I work with a shopping center in Denver that defines its purpose as: *to create promoters of [the shopping center]*. This is a very effective purpose statement or vision because it is simple and concrete. Similar to the Zappos example, every shopping center employee can understand and remember it.

A lack of clarity of purpose exists whenever employees know what to do and how to do it, but do not know why they are doing it. Most often, this is the case.

When I ask five employees with the same job title what they do and how they do it, 80 percent of the responses are similar. This is no surprise since these employees are simply describing their job functions. However, when I ask the same five employees why (from the organization's perspective) they do it, 80 percent of the responses differ.

Most of the time, an organization's "why" is unknown to its employees. Or, the "why" is known but is misunderstood or misinterpreted. There are a variety of reasons for this incongruence, including lack of communication, awareness, understanding, credibility, or interest.

Let's say the organization's purpose (its "why") is reflected in this vision statement:

We will strive to provide exceptional customer service to our customers, coworkers, vendors, and other stakeholders in order to create promoters of our company.

That may be the organization's *stated* purpose—you know, the one that is framed and displayed in the executive offices and perhaps is referenced during the company's new-hire orientation—but it cannot inspire employees unless it is reflected in the culture, policies, and practices of the company, and unless it is brought to life daily in the words and actions of company leaders.

In his book *Start With Why*, Simon Sinek writes:

To inspire starts with the clarity of WHY ... When a WHY is clear, those who share that belief will be drawn to it and maybe want to take part in bringing it to life ... Average companies give their people something to work on ... (The best) organizations give their people something to work toward.

What are your people working toward?

Although it didn't come up during my informal interview with the supermarket employee, the essence of his job role might be to create promoters of his supermarket. In order to create promoters, the employee must execute his job functions in addition to demonstrating job essence. There are countless ways to achieve this, such as:

- Expressing genuine interest in customers
- Displaying a sense of urgency
- Paying attention to detail
- Anticipating the needs of customers
- Conveying authentic enthusiasm for serving customers

Table 1-1 shows examples of job function and job essence for a supermarket employee.

Job function is indicated in job descriptions, policies, procedures, protocol, and checklists. Job essence is reflected in employees' personality, creativity, enthusiasm, passion, and unique flair.

TABLE 1-1 Job Function vs. Job Essence

JOB FUNCTION	JOB ESSENCE
Sack groceries	Express genuine interest in customers
Bring in shopping carts	Display a sense of urgency
Sweep the store	Pay attention to detail
Check prices	Anticipate the needs of customers
Clean up spills	Convey authentic enthusiasm for serving customers

It's not enough to demonstrate attention to job function while ignoring job essence. For example, most parents appreciate a photographer's authentic enthusiasm for photographing their children (job essence), in addition to high-quality photos that reflect proper exposure, aperture, and shutter settings (job function).

It's also insufficient to demonstrate job essence in the absence of job function. An outgoing hotel front desk agent who pleasantly surprises a couple with a spontaneous upgrade to a premium room with ocean views (job essence) ultimately disappoints if she checks them into a dirty room (job function).

In order to provide exceptional customer service and create promoters, employees must exhibit both job function *and* job essence. I recently went to Jimmy John's Gourmet Sandwiches, which emphasizes "freaky fast" speed of service. Upon delivering my order (job function), the employee said, "Sorry you didn't have to wait for that" (job essence). I laughed. By simply interjecting humor, he enlivened what could have been a routine and ordinary transaction.

Figure 1-1 illustrates the necessity of demonstrating both job function (knowledge and skills) and job essence (purpose, one's highest priority at work) in order to provide exceptional customer service and create promoters of a company or brand.

Recently, I spoke with Zane, the manager of a fast-casual restaurant. During our conversation, he shared some of the recurring challenges he faces in trying to elevate customer service at his restaurant.

One frustration he mentioned was the inability of his staff (with the

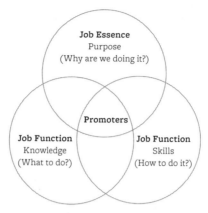

FIGURE 1-1 Three overlapping circles demonstrating job function (knowledge and skills) and job essence (purpose).

exception of one or two "superstars") to consistently provide exceptional customer service. According to Zane, when he challenges employees to "try a little harder" to provide such service, the majority reply, "But I do everything I'm *supposed* to do." This response is telling and may hold the key to whether or not customer service quality will improve at the restaurant.

The employee lament above highlights the mandatory aspect of job functions that are required of employees' job roles—those duties or tasks that are expected by supervisors and customers alike. These are responsibilities that employees are *"supposed* to do." Absent from this remark is anything that is not required, is unexpected, and is voluntary—anything that reflects job essence.

Most employees consistently execute mandatory job functions but inconsistently demonstrate voluntary job essence—behavior that is not required and is often unexpected, actions that employees *choose* to do. This explains why you and I seldom receive exceptional customer service: because employees don't *have* to deliver it. And most don't.

There is one reason why Zane is challenged by staff who consistently deliver hot food hot and cold food cold (job function), but inconsistently express genuine interest in customers or convey authentic enthusiasm in serving them (job essence). It is because most operations, and the supervisors who oversee them, focus predominantly on job functions and the efficiencies associated with them in order to reduce costs and increase profits.

In Zane's restaurant, it's not uncommon for employees to receive feedback on and be held accountable to menu knowledge, following procedures, completing their side work, and other job functions. And it's unlikely that a day goes by that he doesn't scrutinize operational metrics associated with job function: average check, food costs, productivity, profitability, etc. That's what managers do, right?

I told Zane that I understand the importance of job function. Really, I do. You can't run a business without it. And you can't provide exceptional customer service without it. No guest at his restaurant wants an undercooked entrée delivered with a smile. But job function is only *half* an employee's job. The other half, job essence—which is often neglected by employees and managers alike—is missing in most employee interactions that customers would describe as routine and transactional.

Managers must remind employees daily through modeling, feedback, pre-shift meetings, etc., that excellence lies not in what's expected and required (what employees are *supposed* to do) but in what's unexpected and voluntary (what employees *choose* to do). These unexpected and voluntary actions include anticipating customers' needs, paying attention to detail, displaying a sense of urgency, and following up.

And therein lies the second truth of exceptional customer service.

Exceptional Customer Service Is Always Voluntary

Consider the illustrations mentioned earlier in this chapter: Does a photographer *have* to convey authentic enthusiasm for photographing children? Of course not. It's optional. Does a hotel front desk agent *have* to provide a pleasant surprise by spontaneously upgrading guests to a premium room with ocean views? No. Her decision is voluntary. What about a sandwich maker at Jimmy John's? Does he *have* to use appropriate humor with his customers? No. His choice to use humor is voluntary.

Most people don't choose to deliver poor customer service. They just don't choose to deliver exceptional customer service. Most employees are content to simply occupy a customer service role and execute job functions, blissfully unaware of the opportunities they forfeit daily to demonstrate job essence by taking the initiative to do the little things that leave big impressions on customers.

I recall once saying to a client, "Exceptional customer service is *always* optional." Upon hearing this, his eyes narrowed as he leaned forward across the conference table. His voice lowered as he retorted, "Not around here! In my building, exceptional customer service is *mandatory*!"

I disagreed but, in his defense, most general managers would say the same thing: "Of course exceptional customer service is *not* optional. We don't permit employees to provide substandard customer service!"

In theory, they're right. But in practice, they're kidding themselves.

The reason that you and I as customers rarely experience the "exceptional" customer service that these business leaders claim is mandatory is *because* it's optional. An employee *chooses* to make eye contact, smile, or add a bit of enthusiasm to her voice.

Can you recall a recent interaction you've had over the phone or face-to-face with an employee who you sensed was apathetic, bored, or indifferent toward serving you? Of course you can. It happens all the time—even in work environments where exceptional customer service is "mandatory."

Employers can mandate many aspects of an employee's job role: the protocol required to complete a task, the employee's wardrobe and grooming standards, or the time the employee begins or ends her shift. But they cannot mandate the attributes that influence whether or not customers receive exceptional service.

An employee's personality, disposition, uniqueness, creativity, or engagement level is determined by the employee, not her employer. She *chooses* to smile. She *chooses* to refuse to banter with a coworker in front of a customer. She *chooses* to go the extra mile to serve a customer.

While employers cannot mandate these attributes, they can hire for them. That's why the companies that consistently produce the highest levels of customer satisfaction also invest the most in their employee selection efforts. Leaders at these companies are not kidding themselves. They recognize that employees *choose* to provide exceptional customer service (or, as is often the case, choose *not* to), and they establish their employee selection criteria accordingly.

Southwest Airlines is a company that is renowned for its highly selective hiring process, which searches for applicants with the perfect blend of energy, humor, team spirit, and self-confidence to match its famously offbeat and customer-obsessed culture.

This colorful, customer-focused culture is showcased in the following true story received from a blog reader:

CASE STUDY: CUSTOMER FOCUS
AT SOUTHWEST AIRLINES

We were traveling on vacation from Denver to Phoenix when Southwest Airlines lived up to its reputation for spontaneous entertainment and pleasing service. (I love the line, "If you are not pleased with our service, we have six emergency exits throughout the plane. Please locate the one nearest you.")

Approximately halfway through the flight, Nancy, the flight attendant, announced on the intercom: "We have a very special guest onboard named Spencer who turned five years old today. Spencer, could you please join us at the front of the cabin?"

As Spencer made his way forward, a bashful little girl who appeared to be about eight years old emerged from behind the flight attendant, toting a flute.

Nancy explained, "Spencer's sister, Elisa, would like to play 'Happy Birthday' for her brother on the flute."

Elisa sporadically blew her best "Happy Birthday" song and the passengers clapped. Then, the whole cabin, led by Nancy, sang the birthday song to Spencer, who delighted in all the attention!

Next, Nancy placed a crown on Spencer's head. The crown was made of clear Scotch tape, Southwest Airlines peanut packets, and red plastic olive skewers.

As King Spencer marched down the aisle proudly, I noticed the crown—an unnecessary, spontaneous, free, yet brilliant example of customer enthusiasm that cannot be mandated but cannot be overvalued.

No doubt, Spencer ate part of his crown before his parents retrieved their bags, but he won't soon forget that flight. Neither will I.

This story illustrates the third truth of exceptional customer service.

Exceptional Customer Service Typically Costs No More to Deliver than Poor Customer Service

It's true. When you break it down to its fundamental components, exceptional customer service typically costs no more to deliver than mediocre customer service (or at least no more than the cost of some peanuts, olive skewers, and Scotch tape).

How much does it cost to express genuine interest in customers or to anticipate their needs? Does it cost more to display a sense of urgency or to pay attention to detail? Do you pay your employees more to smile, to make eye contact, or to add energy to their voices? Of course not. These qualities, in addition to most actions associated with exceptional customer service, are free.

Recall the illustrations mentioned earlier in the chapter. What does it cost the photographer to convey authentic enthusiasm for photographing children? Nothing. Enthusiasm is free. What does it cost the hotel to upgrade the guests to an unoccupied and available premium room with ocean views? There is no cost. This pleasant surprise is free. What about the Jimmy John's employee? What does it cost him to use appropriate humor with his customers? Nothing. A sense of humor is free.

In order to understand what extraordinary customer service is, it is helpful to contrast it with typical customer service quality. Below are five distinctions that separate exceptional customer service from the bland and ordinary service that customers typically receive.

1. **Function vs. Essence.** Exceptional customer service requires that employees both execute job function *and* display job essence. However, most employees are blissfully unaware of the distinction between the two.

2. **Mandatory vs. Voluntary.** Job functions tend to be transactional. They are also required: Employees must perform them. This explains why many customer service experiences are described as process-focused and robotic. Delivering exceptional service is voluntary. It requires a deliberate choice by the service provider. This explains why you and I as customers seldom receive it.

3. **Obligation vs. Opportunity.** Employees are obligated to execute mandatory job functions. They don't have a choice. It's what they were hired to do. Just read their job descriptions. It's all right there. These same employees, however, have an opportunity to display voluntary job essence: to express genuine interest in customers, convey authentic enthusiasm for serving others, provide pleasant surprises, etc. But these opportunities are often squandered in the name of operational efficiency or some other management priority.

4. **Results vs. Relationships.** Mandatory job functions that employees are obligated to execute yield predictable results that are measured and scrutinized by management. If employees do receive feedback on their job performance, it generally relates to job functions. By contrast, voluntary job essence that employees have an opportunity to demonstrate develop relationships with customers that inspire loyalty, repeat purchases, higher profit margins, and enthusiastic referrals.

5. **Cost vs. No Cost (or negligible cost).** Mandatory job functions that employees are obligated to execute in order to achieve certain results require compensation. This is what they are paid to do. Voluntary job essence that employees elect to display in order to develop relationships with customers costs nothing—or the cost is negligible when compared to the lifetime value of a loyal customer. There is no additional cost for a service provider to smile, offer a sincere and specific compliment, or share unique knowledge.

A typical manager's routine involves job functions, mandates, obligations, results, and costs. It's no wonder customer service tends to be transactional and uninspired.

What is needed is a different approach—one that reinforces job essence, voluntary decisions to delight customers, capitalizing on opportunities, building relationships, and a recognition that it costs no more to smile and greet customers than it does to ignore them.

Table 1-2 distinguishes between attributes of ordinary and extraordinary customer service.

TABLE 1–2 Ordinary Service vs. Extraordinary Service

ORDINARY SERVICE	EXTRAORDINARY SERVICE
Job functions: The duties or tasks associated with a job role	*Job essence:* An employee's highest priority at work (i.e., to create delighted customers!)
Mandatory: Job functions are required	*Voluntary:* The decision to express genuine interest in a customer, convey authentic enthusiasm, or go the extra mile is a choice
Obligation: Employees are obligated to execute job functions	*Opportunity:* Employees have the opportunity to do the "little things" that will leave lasting positive impressions on customers
Achieving results: Executing job functions produces predictable results that are usually objective and easy to quantify	*Building relationships:* Demonstrating job essence develops relationships (this is generally subjective and difficult to quantify)
Cost: Employees are paid to execute job functions	*Little or no cost:* Taking the initiative to leave a lasting positive impression costs nothing
Indifferent: Describes customer service that is bland, uneventful, and forgettable	*Different:* Describes customer service that is unique, refreshing, and memorable
Efficient: Doing more things more quickly	*Effective:* Doing fewer things well
Transactional: Process-focused, treating each customer like the last customer	*Experiential:* People-focused, treating each customer as an individual
Short-term view: "How much did we make on that transaction?"	*Long-term view:* "What is the lifetime value of a delighted customer?"
Yields passives: Satisfied but unenthusiastic customers who can be easily wooed by the competition	*Yields promoters:* Loyal customers who are less price-sensitive, have higher repurchase rates, and account for 80–90% of positive word of mouth about a company or brand

Typical customer service is routine, expected, and ordinary. It is process-focused and transactional and tends to yield passive customers, who are defined by Bain & Company as "satisfied but unenthusiastic customers who can be easily wooed by the competition." You can't build a business on a foundation of passive customers who base their buying decisions on convenience or whether or not they are able to obtain your product or service at a discount.

Employees who work in these environments tend to maintain the status quo by doing what is expected of them—what they are told to do by management. It's not uncommon for these employees to describe their jobs as boring and routine. In the absence of job essence, all that exists is a transaction. Transactions are not memorable. Transactional service does not make a lasting positive impression or inspire loyalty.

Early in this chapter, I observed that when asked to describe what their job entails, most employees list only job functions—the duties or tasks associated with their job roles. Why is it that employees rarely mention job essence?

Consider this: Job function is results-oriented. Managers are interested in results. Job function is doing what you are told. Managers appreciate compliance. Job function is doing what's expected. Managers don't like surprises.

Until managers actively model, recognize, and reward job essence, achieving results will take priority over establishing relationships, compliance will trump initiative, and customer service will be characterized by routine and predictable transactions.

Energy flows where attention goes. And most employees see job function being recognized and rewarded over job essence.

For instance, let's go back to the supermarket employee we met at the beginning of this chapter. Let's assume that during his new-hire orientation program, he was told how important it was to provide exceptional customer service. Perhaps he read a mission statement, was shown a poster, or was given a button to wear that touted the company's customer service slogan. He was also made aware of his job duties that include gathering the stray shopping carts from the parking lot.

Being enthusiastic about his new job and wanting to perform well, the employee is conscientious when bagging groceries. He is careful to handle delicate items such as bread and eggs gently and to bag frozen food together to prevent it from thawing too quickly. He also insists on helping customers to their cars—especially when the weather is bad—even though most of his coworkers avoid this step.

During his first several weeks in his new position, the employee is routinely approached by his manager, who asks, "Hey, why are there so many carts in the parking lot?" But he never receives any feedback about the exceptional customer service he provides to shoppers.

So he's conflicted. He says, "During orientation, they told me how important it was to take care of the customer. I try to do that, but no one seems to notice or care. The only thing I ever receive feedback on is the number of shopping carts in the parking lot."

It doesn't take him long to learn that the way he's going to earn the favor of his manager is by spending more time in the parking lot, away from customers, retrieving shopping carts.

I recognize that job function is necessary—even critical (i.e., the shopping carts must be retrieved from the parking lot, and the floor needs to be swept periodically)—but it does not represent the *totality* of an employee's job role! It represents only *half* of it. The other half of his job, which is often neglected, is job essence. His highest priority at work is to create promoters.

When employees are made aware of the essence of their jobs and it is reinforced (i.e., modeled, recognized, and rewarded) by their immediate supervisors, then customer service quality improves, fewer eggs get broken, and more lasting positive impressions are made on customers.

GETTING FROM ORDINARY TO EXTRAORDINARY

- There are two aspects of every employee's job role: job function and job essence. *Job function* refers to the duties or tasks associated with a job role. *Job essence* is the most critical aspect—the highest priority—of every service industry employee's job role.
- Job function includes employees' job knowledge (what they do) and job skills (how they do it). Most employees are aware of their responsibility to execute job function and are proficient in this aspect of their work.

- Job essence includes employees' motivation (why they do it). Employees are less clear about this dimension of their job roles, mainly because they are focused on job function.
- Job function is indicated in job descriptions, policies, procedures, protocol, and checklists.
- Job essence is reflected in employees' personality, creativity, enthusiasm, passion, and unique flair.
- A promoter, as defined by the firm Bain & Company, is a customer who is less price-sensitive, has higher repurchase rates, and is responsible for 80 to 90 percent of the positive word of mouth about a company or brand.
- The first truth of exceptional customer service is that it reflects job essence.
- The second truth of exceptional customer service is that it is always voluntary.
- The third truth of exceptional customer service is that it typically costs no more to deliver than average service. In other words, it's free.
- While employees consistently execute mandatory job functions for which they are paid, they inconsistently demonstrate voluntary job essence for which there is little or no additional cost to the employer.
- The reason that you and I as customers inconsistently receive exceptional customer service is because it's voluntary. It's left to chance. Employees don't *have* to deliver it, and most don't.
- Most people don't choose to deliver poor customer service. They just don't choose to deliver exceptional customer service.
- Energy flows where attention goes, and most employees see job function being recognized and rewarded over job essence. Job function is results-oriented. Managers are interested in results. Job function is doing what you are told. Managers appreciate compliance. Job function is doing what's expected. Managers don't like surprises.
- Until managers actively model, recognize, and reward job essence, achieving results will take priority over establishing relationships, compliance will trump initiative, and customer service will be characterized by routine and predictable actions.

Applying Three Truths of Exceptional Customer Service

In the space provided, record examples of how you can apply concepts from the chapter to raise customer service quality that you deliver or influence from ordinary to extraordinary!

ORDINARY	EXTRAORDINARY
Make employees aware of the mandatory job functions for which they are responsible to execute.	Reveal to employees that their jobs are made up of two parts: job function and job essence.

Part Two

SEVEN SIMPLE WAYS TO RAISE CUSTOMER SERVICE

2

Express Genuine Interest

Have you ever heard someone in a committed relationship say that he no longer loves the other person? When questioned, he might say, "I've tried. Really I have. But the *love* just isn't there."

It's no wonder the love isn't there because love (the noun) *is a result* of love (the verb). In the absence of *demonstrating* love for another person, there's only a relationship—an association, an existence together. Heck, I have *that* type of relationship with my mailman.

In a committed relationship, it's not sufficient to view love as a noun—a mercurial feeling that vacillates between satisfied and unsatisfied. Love must be demonstrated. Love requires action. Love is a verb.

It's the same with customer service. Too many service providers view service as a noun—a role, function, or department. As a result, customer service is objectified and lifeless.

Last year, I spoke with a friend who oversees the training of 4,500 call center employees for a Fortune 100 company. He mentioned that these employees are required to express empathy during phone calls pertaining to warranty issues or other repairs. He said that if an employee simply repeats the customer's problem back to her, then that would satisfy the requirement to express empathy during a call audit. In other words, if a customer calls in and says, "My washing machine stopped working," then all the employee would have to say is, "I'm sorry to hear that your washing machine stopped working" in order to receive full credit for expressing empathy.

However, my friend was not satisfied with this protocol. He proposed that genuine empathy might look more like a call center employee detecting a crying baby in the background and then saying, "I hear a crying baby. Would you like me to look into the availability of a service appointment for tomorrow and call you back in a few minutes?"

Service must be demonstrated. Service requires action. Service is a verb.

Merely going through the motions, whether in a committed relationship or with a customer, results in a routine, predictable, and lifeless association. This opens the door for a competitor.

Do not view service as a noun. Do not see "serving customers" as performing a role or function—whether or not it involves a script, a checklist, or a requirement to "express empathy."

The opposite of action is inaction. (If you ever had to load your own suitcase in the trunk of a taxicab and get your own door while the driver remained comfortably seated behind the wheel, then you know what I'm talking about.) Action is voluntary. A service provider *chooses* to demonstrate initiative.

The opposite of initiative is indifference. Often, employees are indifferent toward the needs of customers. Like the taxi driver who remains behind the wheel, they miss opportunities to provide exceptional service by failing to observe their surroundings, anticipate needs, or display a sense of urgency. Opportunities to make lasting positive impressions on customers are forfeited, along with their loyalty and future spending.

To illustrate the attribute of initiative at work, consider the example of tennis professional Matt Previdi.

CASE STUDY: A TENNIS PRO'S INITIATIVE

My tennis club recently hosted the Colorado Classic Pro Am Tennis Tournament. Because of the caliber of players, tennis professional Matt Previdi was made available as an on-site racket stringer by SOLINCO, one of the tournament sponsors.

I happened to be at the club during the tournament. Matt, while stringing a racket behind the tennis desk, noticed (verb) as I was adjusting my elbow brace and asked (verb), "Tennis elbow?"

I responded, "Yes. I've been dealing with tendonitis for the past seven months or so."

He paused (verb) his work, stepped (verb) out in front of the stringing machine, and asked (verb) to see (verb) one of my rackets. I handed it to him, and he began (verb) to test (verb) its tension by smacking (verb) the racket against the palm of his hand. After a few seconds, he determined (verb) that my strings and tension were likely a contributing factor to my tendonitis.

After asking (verb) a few probing questions about my style of play, he advised (verb) me to consider a string with greater elasticity to absorb more of the ball's energy and suggested (verb) I reduce the tension at which I string my rackets.

As my hitting partner arrived, Matt offered (verb) me his racket and said (verb), "Try my racket today. It's comparable in weight to your racket, and the strings and tension will be a lot easier on your elbow. Afterward, let me know what you think."

Borrowed racket in hand, I headed to the court with my partner. Later that afternoon, I approached Matt and said, "You were right! The combination of flexible string and reduced tension was much easier on my elbow. I wish I'd discovered it sooner."

I then handed Matt all three of my rackets, asked him to cut out the existing strings (two of which were new sets of strings), and replace them with the recommended strings at the reduced tension.

Upon receiving my rackets, Matt said (verb), "Steve, I did (verb) a little scouting on your game and noticed (verb) that you tend to hit out rather than up. By reducing the string tension to relieve stress on your elbow, the ball's going to have more 'pop' coming off the racket. If you continue to swing out at the ball rather than up through the ball, you're going to hit a lot of balls long."

Amazing. Although he was swamped with requests to restring rackets, he had taken (verb) the time to watch (verb) me hit in order to verify (verb) that his recommendations matched my style of play.

If you're curious, the cost for me to string three rackets was $111. Ordinarily, I string my rackets elsewhere. So, that's $111 in added sales created (verb) as a result of an engaged employee taking (verb) the initiative to observe (verb) his surroundings, express (verb) genuine interest in the customer, and provide (verb) exceptional customer service.

Again, service, like love, is a verb. As such, it requires action and effort and it must be demonstrated. When done well—consistently, with genuine care and concern—you make a lasting positive impression and ensure that your "customer" only has eyes for you.

While there is not necessarily an order to the seven simple ways to raise your customer service, it's no accident that the first behavior is to express genuine interest.

How to Express Genuine Interest

Although several of the behaviors discussed below are situational and may not apply to every customer service encounter, every interaction provides an opportunity to express genuine interest.

Expressing genuine interest requires going beyond the basic customer service expectations of the job role. Ordinarily, these basics consist of the behaviors that satisfy most customers' fundamental expectations for face-to-face interactions with service providers: smiling, making eye contact, and adding energy to one's voice. But employees can also express genuine interest through work habits such as paying attention to detail and displaying a sense of urgency.

Regardless of how it's exhibited, expressing genuine interest in customers requires that employees demonstrate initiative and take action—as Matt Previdi modeled. There are many ways to accomplish this:

- Offer personalized greetings
- Use names
- Practice assertive hospitality
- Ask questions
- Cosset
- Anticipate needs
- Remember preferences
- Pay attention to detail
- Display a sense of urgency
- Solicit feedback
- Offer personal farewells
- Follow up on service

Offer Personalized Greetings

Do you pay attention to the greetings you receive as a customer?

I do.

Recently, when I pulled up to the Krispy Kreme drive-through window, my greeting was: "$16.65."

That was it. I was greeted with the total cost of my order.

At Dairy Queen, the greeting was no better. After waiting in line for several minutes, my wife and I and our four children made our way to the front of the line. Looking at the "scrumpdillyicious" pictures on the menus suspended above the counter, my youngest children could hardly contain their enthusiasm! Their eyes, wide with wonder, darted from one delectable menu image to the next. They smiled and began to giggle as they realized it was now their turn to order and that, within minutes, they would have their frosty treats in hand! Smiling in response to my children's excitement, I looked up to face the counter employee. In sharp contrast to my children's faces, her facial expression was indifferent—even serious. Her greeting consisted of, "Do you know what you want?"

Here are several other "greetings" that I have received lately:

- "For here or to go?"
- "Paper or plastic?"
- "Two for dinner?"
- "Checking in?"
- "Next?"
- "Phone number?" (when I dropped off dry cleaning and the employee wanted to locate my account)

All too often, customer greetings and references become transactional. Customers lose their unique identities as they dutifully conform to employees' dogmatic focus on job function. Below are several examples from my own experience, accompanied by alternatives that express genuine interest in customers.

> **Greeting:** *"'05 Expedition?"* This was how I was addressed by the service technician in the waiting area the last time I brought my SUV in for service at the dealership. This oversight was avoidable. My name was printed on the service order. This particular technician just fell into the bad habit of favoring vehicles' names over customers'.
> **Alternative:** *"Mr. Curtin?"*

> **Greeting:** *"Internet trouble?"* This was the greeting I received from a technician when I opened my guest room door at a conference center in New Jersey.
> **Alternative:** *"Good evening, Mr. Curtin. I understand that you're unable to connect to the Internet. May I come in and take a look?"*

> **Reference:** *"12 C"* as in, *"12 C needs a pillow."* I understand what's going on here. Flight attendants are busy, and customers are demanding. Shortcuts like these provide the efficiency needed to process more customers in less time, thus making everybody happy, right? Well, not everybody . . . We know from con-

sumer research that customers appreciate being recognized as customers—preferably by name.

Alternative: *"The passenger in seat 12 C needs a pillow."* Or, if the flight attendant has the flight manifest in her possession, she can add the name to personalize the request further: *"Mr. Curtin, in seat 12 C, needs a pillow."*

Reference: *"Room 812"* as in, *"Room 812 needs more towels."* This was what a Kansas City hotel representative said as I stood a few feet away from him on the other side of the counter in the lobby.

Alternative: *"Our guest in room 812 needs more towels."* Or, if he had—or had access to—the guest's name, then he could include it: *"Mr. Curtin, our guest in room 812, needs more towels."*

Sometimes the greetings are perfectly acceptable but lose their appeal after you hear the same rote salutation repeated again and again to customers who arrive after you.

My boys are big LEGO fans and, whenever we're at the mall, we make it a point to stop in to see the latest building sets on display. The LEGO Store routinely has an employee stationed near the entrance to greet customers as they arrive. At this particular store, the employee's greeting is, "Welcome to the LEGO Store. Who gets the LEGO set today?" Although appropriate, this greeting becomes mechanical, even annoying, after you hear it repeated ten times with the same cadence during your first minute inside the store.

Consider spending five to ten minutes during your next pre-shift or department meeting identifying examples of customer greetings and references from your world of work that sound transactional or rehearsed. Explore alternatives that express genuine interest in your customers and convey sincere appreciation for their patronage. Then hold each other accountable. Look for opportunities to catch employees doing it right, and coach in situations where they fall short of the standard. As managers, recognize that you too are accountable to consistently model the standard.

Set the standard high. Avoid using generic labels when greeting or referring to customers. Use customers' names whenever possible. In doing so, you are expressing genuine interest in your customers and re-inforcing their uniqueness and personal importance.

Use Names

Names can be used in circumstances other than greetings and references. A client recently asked me, "How can I *fake* that I know a customer's name? I have a thousand regulars in my restaurant each week and can't possibly remember all of their names."

I recognize that remembering names is not always easy. I'm the first to admit that I often forget a name just seconds after hearing it—especially if I'm being introduced to a group of people. Recalling names takes real effort and—for many of us—if we're not intentional about it, we miss opportunities to capture and use them.

We already know that people love hearing the sound of their own name. And when they are greeted by name, especially in a setting where they are customers, it affirms their importance as customers—and the value they bring to the business through personal spending, referrals, and loyalty.

My response to my client was this: "Rather than mislead customers by faking that you know their names, why not make the effort instead to learn them?"

I then shared with her some advice I had recently given to my ten-year-old son, Cole, while he was attending a tennis camp with a dozen or so peers after school. On the drive home from camp one evening, I asked Cole the name of the boy he'd been hitting with during the final drill. To my surprise, he had no idea what the boy's name was.

When I reminded Cole that learning and using others' names expresses genuine interest in them, conveys respect, and affirms their personal importance, he complained that there were many kids and that learning all their names would be difficult.

So, together, we devised some strategies that he could use to help remember the names of the other players at camp. We started with the names of players he already knew. There were two: Paris and Rachel. (Both girls. Mmm . . .)

I asked him to describe Paris, and he said she was tall. Then I asked him what came to mind when he thought of the name "Paris." He said, "Paris, France."

Next, I asked him if there was anything tall in Paris, France. He said, "The Eiffel Tower."

Then Cole said, "I get it! To help remember her name, I can think of the Eiffel Tower in Paris, France."

I mentioned that this is an example of a *mnemonic*—a learning device that assists in remembering something—but Cole was already thinking of a way to help remember Rachel's name. He said, "When I see Rachel again, I'll remember that her name is the same as my cousin Rachel in Sioux Falls!"

"That's great, Cole!" I said. "You're using an *association* you're very familiar with to help remember the name of someone you've recently met."

The last suggestion I gave to Cole was to *repeat* the name of the person he was meeting several times during the initial introduction. For example: "Rachel? I have a cousin named Rachel. My name is Cole. Nice to meet you, Rachel!"

There is no easy way to remember names. But it is possible to facilitate learning names by using mnemonics, associations, and repetition. When employees invest the time and effort to learn customers' names, they are expressing genuine interest in their customers and reinforcing their personal importance.

Practice Assertive Hospitality

To approach customers means to practice *assertive hospitality*, which is being present to serve customers without suffocating them. Assertive hospitality is not aggressive. The used car salesman approach, whether you are selling cars, fragrance, clothing, or some other product or service, is a turnoff to most customers who appreciate being able to look, smell, hear, touch, and taste without being rushed or hounded by an overbearing employee. The most effective restaurant servers choreograph their table approaches to verify meat temperatures, remove used side plates, refill water glasses, etc., just as the most professional clothing salespeople make themselves available to prospective customers while allowing them time and space to browse.

Employees should not wait for customers to acknowledge them. Instead, they should be assertive, interested, and engaged and should acknowledge their customers first. This requires initiative, which may be the single most decisive attribute that distinguishes exceptional customer service providers from the rest.

A great way to reinforce the importance of practicing assertive hospitality is by introducing the 15 × 5 Rule. This rule suggests making eye contact and smiling when a customer is within a distance of approximately fifteen feet, and adding an appropriate greeting (e.g., "Good morning," "Good afternoon") when within approximately five feet of a customer. The 15 × 5 Rule is a noninvasive way for employees to acknowledge customers, demonstrate that they are engaged, and reinforce their willingness and availability to serve.

Ask Questions

Asking questions is an effective way to express genuine interest in customers and build the rapport necessary to establish loyalty.

During the morning rush hour, Starbucks baristas can expect a line of time-pressed commuters waiting to place their orders. That's okay. The baristas don't need to have long conversations at the register. But they can simply express interest by saying something like, "Off to work?" or, "Big plans today?" These types of questions aren't intended to inspire long conversations that undermine service to waiting customers. They're simply intended to express genuine interest in the customer.

Here's another example of asking questions to express interest. Two years ago, I delivered the opening conference keynote address for a group at the Mirage Resort & Casino in Las Vegas. As I stood in the hotel's taxicab line later that morning, I observed a doorman named Folk doing a masterful job of engaging guests with questions while remaining attentive to the fact that there was a continual line of waiting customers.

As I progressed to the front of the line, Folk whistled for a waiting cab to pull forward. Even his natural whistle was different, melodic and original, and reflected his unique style and flair.

As he took my suitcase, he asked, "Are you an NFL fan?"

"Yes," I answered.

He said, "In the Detroit game, catch or no-catch?" (He was referring to a controversial incomplete pass ruling that went against the Detroit Lions in their loss to the Chicago Bears the previous Sunday.) I told him that I'd heard about the controversy but had not seen the play so I really couldn't comment.

Before closing the cab door, Folk asked, "Where are you from?"

"Denver," I replied.

Smiling, he said, "Oh, a Broncos fan! Come back and see us!"

Not only did Folk execute his job function efficiently, he also demonstrated job essence by asking questions as a way to express genuine interest in hotel guests and make a lasting positive impression.

Cosset

Cosset means to pamper or treat with excessive indulgence. I think of cosseting as a higher form of expressing genuine interest in a customer. It's the subtle difference between handing customers' purchases over the counter and walking *around* the counter to hand them directly to customers, as Nordstrom salespeople do. It's really nothing more than an extra step—a gesture of appreciation and respect. And it doesn't go unnoticed.

Cosseting is also seen in the way that exceptional coat check attendants handle guests' coats. They are intentional about not mangling jacket lapels as they situate the coats between other coats. This is quite refreshing behavior when the norm is for attendants to jam coats in wherever there is room without regard for the garments' appearance.

It's also evident in the way conscientious grocery store sackers handle customers' purchases. They take care to protect fragile produce, soft bread, and delicate eggs as they bag the groceries, as opposed to indiscriminately cramming as much as they can into the bag.

Here's an example of an employee missing an opportunity to treat the customer well. Over Memorial Day weekend, I brought my son Cooper to a two-day basketball camp in Lakewood, Colorado. The first day, we stopped by an independent coffee shop where I ordered a double espresso in a ceramic cup for dine-in.

After a mechanical transaction executed by an indifferent employee, Cooper and I took seats among the open tables. A few minutes later, I heard the barista call out, "Double espresso!"

When I looked up, I saw my espresso order sitting on the far end of the bar. I got up, walked the twenty feet or so to the end of the bar, and retrieved my order. The barista was talking with two other employees behind the counter. I thought about the opportunity she missed to "go the extra mile" (or, at least, the extra twenty feet) and deliver the order to my table. (For the record, there were three employees and a total of five customers in the coffee shop, with no one in line waiting to be served.)

By going just a little out of their way to serve customers, employees are expressing genuine interest in serving them. By not delivering the espresso to my table, the barista who prepared my order missed an opportunity to cosset her guest.

Cynical employees might say, "Come on, you're perfectly capable of getting up and walking twenty feet to get your own espresso." And they're right—as my actions demonstrated. Similarly, a guest in your home is capable of fetching her own cup of coffee, but my hunch is that most of you would insist on serving her. And if you don't, over time, I suspect you'll have fewer guests in your home.

It's no different at the local coffee shop. Over time, it too will have fewer guests to serve—starting with me. We chose not to return to that coffee shop on the second day of the camp.

Anticipate Needs

Customers appreciate it when you take the initiative to anticipate and fulfill their needs without being asked to do so. Sometimes it's something simple like a hotel doorman getting the door for guests as they approach or a restaurant hostess providing crayons and kids' menus to occupy children until the food comes. Other times, it's more involved, such as when an airport director advises concessionaires to extend their hours in order to accommodate airline passengers when there is an influx of weather-related flight delays.

Anticipating needs requires attentiveness, organization, care, and concern for the comfort and well-being of customers. The very act of anticipating implies that it requires forethought. Just as one would plan ahead to meet the needs of dinner party guests by, for instance, accommodating dietary restrictions, so should businesses prepare to meet the needs of their customers.

In a supermarket, this may include strategically locating stacks of hand baskets toward the rear of the store. This way, they can be picked up by customers who neglected to get a basket when they entered the store but have found that they had gathered more groceries than expected.

Many public parks offer biodegradable pet waste bags as an amenity for pet owners. By making the waste bags available, the park is serving its community by anticipating the needs of pet owners and helping to provide a clean park for visitors.

I know of a very successful retail salesperson who keeps her eye on the society page of her local paper. Many of her customers attend the same charity events and galas, and she has become known for discreetly keeping track of who buys what for which event. When someone wants a dress that she knows has already been bought by another woman, she says, "I'm very sorry, that dress has been sold," and she guides the customer to something else. By doing so, she is anticipating her clients' need for exclusivity and uniqueness in the dresses they wear to society events.

Sometimes, anticipating a customer's needs is not planned ahead of time but happens in the moment. If a customer in a shopping mall is standing in front of a directory with a perplexed look on her face, a passing custodial employee or security officer can assume that she may have a question about the availability or location of a particular store, and he can provide the information she needs.

Remember Preferences

Remembering customer preferences requires effort. Baristas and bartenders must be intentional about committing a regular customer's drink order to memory. Even when using software to capture and store customer preferences, there is only an empty record until an employee enters data. The more specific and current the data is, the greater the opportunity to provide exceptional customer service.

Last year, I had dinner with a client, Victor, and his wife at Summer Winter in Burlington, Massachusetts. Although six months had elapsed since Victor's last visit to the restaurant, when he said to his wife, "I wish I could remember the name of the Pinot Noir we had the last time we were here," the waiter responded, "I believe it was the 2009 Lemelson Vineyards Thea's Selection Oregon Pinot Noir."

Surprised, Victor said, "I think you're right! We really enjoyed that wine. I'd like to order the same bottle tonight."

After the waiter left the table, I remarked that he had a really good memory, to which Victor replied, "Or really good software." Either way, the result is the same: By recalling customer preferences, service providers are expressing genuine interest in customers while making lasting positive impressions.

Incidentally, I later phoned the restaurant to determine what software it was utilizing to capture and archive guest preferences. As it turns out, Summer Winter does not use software for that purpose. Its employees simply practice good old-fashioned customer service!

Pay Attention to Detail

I used to work for a hotel general manager who was fond of saying, "If you close your eyes once, you've lowered your standards." He said this in the context of quality and consistency, encouraging managers to refuse to overlook important details, ignore spills in the back aisle, or walk past debris on the floor expecting someone else to take care it. At one point, I had earned the nickname "Hoover" (as in the vacuum company) because of my compulsion to pick up tiny pieces of paper I spotted on the floor. It's not that I was a "neat freak." I just didn't want to let my general manager down, or worse, let myself down by lowering my personal standards.

One aspect of my current consulting business is mystery shopping services. When you conduct a mystery shop, you uncover many details pertaining to individual clients' criteria for a successful customer experience. Sometimes, these details have to do with cleanliness. Other times, these details pertain to following established protocol for cash handling, transferring phone calls, or completing some other transaction.

Whenever I encounter employees who are nervous about having the quality of their work evaluated by a mystery shopper, I tell them, "If you do it right every time, you'll be doing it right at the right time." And by paying attention to detail, your odds of doing it right increase dramatically.

I enjoy taking my family to On The Border Mexican Grill & Cantina. In fact, I look forward to it. The restaurants are clean, the food quality is excellent, and the value for price paid is fair.

My wife, however, has one problem with On The Border. This single issue has caused us to choose competing restaurants on a number of occasions. Her problem: Servers consistently overlook details and allow tables to become overrun with used side plates, chip bowls, and ramekins of salsa, sour cream, and guacamole.

During college, my wife worked at her father's restaurant and learned early on to never leave a table empty-handed when there were items to be cleared. By observing their surroundings and paying attention to detail, the most effective servers would spot discarded straw wrappers, empty appetizer plates, or depleted breadbaskets. By taking care of such things, the servers kept the dining tables neat and orderly.

Servers at our local On The Border restaurant appear to be completely unaware of this protocol. With four children, the dishes add up. It's not long before our table surface disappears beneath a pile of used plates, dirty napkins, and other clutter. Near the end of the meal, even if we had room for dessert, we wouldn't have the space for it.

One of the benefits customers cite when justifying the added cost to dine out is the ability to enjoy a dining experience they would otherwise be incapable of reproducing at home. My family is perfectly capable of producing a cluttered dinner table at home. When we dine out, we appreciate an attentive server who maintains an orderly table.

Sure, I could stack the used plates, move them to the side of the table, and request their removal (I do this routinely at On The Border), but I don't want to. That's why I'm out to eat. If I'm going to accept responsibility for stacking plates and clearing table space, I'll save my money and eat at home.

Restaurant guests appreciate being looked after—even pampered. Servers—by observing their surroundings, paying attention to detail, and committing to never leave a cluttered table empty-handed—reduce table congestion and maybe, just maybe, make room for dessert!

Display a Sense of Urgency

Employees who display a sense of urgency inspire confidence in customers. Sometimes, a sense of urgency is conveyed using words or phrases such as "Absolutely" or "Right away" in response to customer requests.

Other times, urgency is demonstrated in actions—such as when employees move with alacrity, showing a readiness or eagerness to assist customers. Valet parkers who hustle into the parking lot and emerge a minute later with your vehicle inspire larger tips than valet parkers who are observed walking in the direction of the parking lot while preoccupied with their smartphones. In the same way, standing at attention behind a counter, ready to serve, conveys a sense of urgency whereas leaning against a partition or counter coveys indifference and undermines a sense of urgency.

I once took a cab from McCarran International Airport in Las Vegas to my hotel on the Strip. About ten minutes into the drive, I struck up a conversation with the cab driver about the purpose of my trip—to speak to an insurance group about customer service.

He asked me a question or two about customer service, and one of the comments I made was that exceptional customer service is not usually the result of one big thing. It's often the result of many "little things" done exceptionally well.

To illustrate my point, I said, "For instance, while you sat comfortably in the driver's seat, I slid the door open, stowed my bag, and then, once I was seated inside, I had to reposition myself in order to reach back and pull the door closed. I managed, but my point is that you missed an opportunity to provide exceptional customer service. Had you hustled out of your seat to assist me, I would have noticed."

I went on to say that if he chose to take my advice and demonstrate a sense of urgency to stow luggage and open and close the door for passengers, then I believed his tips would increase by 20 percent.

He appeared interested.

I asked him if he kept a record of his tips, and he said that he had been driving a cab for only about four weeks. He said that previously, he was a commercial truck driver, but he was terminated after his third driving incident. (At this point, I made sure I had buckled my seat belt.) He estimated that he made about $40 a day in tips. I told him to apply my suggestion for a day and see whether or not his tip average increased.

I said, "Now, you still have to be competent. Customers won't appreciate that you got their doors if you drive them around in circles. You must demonstrate knowledge of the area, drive safely, and be polite."

I have no idea whether or not he applied my advice, but I do know this: Customers take notice and appreciate it when service providers hustle and demonstrate a sense of urgency when serving them. And, when gratuities are involved, this translates into bigger tips!

Solicit Feedback

Two years ago, I stayed in a New York City hotel where I was scheduled to deliver a presentation. Shortly before my talk, I met the hotel's beverage director, who asked if I had any feedback for him pertaining to the hotel's food and beverage outlets. I shared a couple of pieces of feedback and then added that I was surprised that, with a selection of a dozen different beers on tap in the bar, there was no pale ale option.

He responded, "Have you tried the Brooklyn Lager?"

I said, "Scott, I've tried Brooklyn Lager, but I'm interested in an ale, not a lager." Unswayed, he said, "I'd stock a pale ale, but the kegs are $169 each—which is a lot more than the others."

"Scott," I said, "I've never once stopped a bartender from pouring a beer in order to confirm the price beforehand. Neither will your customers."

When you solicit feedback from customers, don't marginalize their responses or sound defensive. If you do, they stop giving you meaningful feedback and just say what they think you want to hear—if they say anything at all.

I recalled my conversation with Scott a few months later and, out of curiosity, phoned the hotel bar to see if pale ale had been added to the beer menu. To Scott's credit, he had listened to his customer and added a tap for Captain Lawrence Pale Ale. According to the bartender I spoke with, "It's a good seller."

Offer Personal Farewells

Just as many greetings are transactional, farewells too have a tendency to become rehearsed and lifeless with repetition. Below are some of the impersonal farewells I've received in the past.

Farewell from the cashier handing me my order at the Krispy Kreme drive-through: *"Your receipt's in the bag."* That was my farewell. Nothing more. This employee seemed to prioritize efficiency (processing more customers more quickly) over effectiveness (making lasting positive impressions on his customers).
Alternative: *"Thank you. Come back and see us!"*

Farewell from the cashier speaking into the register phone handset: *"I'm at register six. Do you want me to bank out on register seven?"* After I had spent $62.15 on groceries at Albertsons, that was my farewell. I was completely ignored by the cashier as he chose to focus on his real priority: getting the hell out of there.
Alternative: *"Thank you very much. We'll see you next time!"*

Below are several other transactional and dismissive "farewells" that I frequently receive:

- *"Here you go."* This is said as I'm handed a bag, a pizza, or a receipt.
- *"Next?"* Oh, I guess that means you and I are done and I should skedaddle . . .
- *"No problem."* So I should be relieved that I didn't cause you too much trouble by giving your company my business?
- *"You're welcome."* I always find it to be ironic that, most often, it is the customer who thanks the cashier—apparently for accepting her money—when it should be the other way around.
- *"Do you want your receipt with you or in the bag?"*

Appropriate farewells appear to have left the repertoires of most customer-facing employees in the service industry, having been reduced to robotic send-offs signaling the end of a transaction rather than expressing gratitude for a sale. Employees must recognize that whether face-to-face, over the phone, or online, a farewell is incomplete without adding, "Thank you!"

Follow Up on Service

Here's an example of an employee following up on service in all the right ways.

CASE STUDY: THE COMMITTED
CAR WASH ATTENDANT

Last fall, I brought my car into Car Wash Express in Centennial, Colorado, to remove the window paint my son had used over the weekend to decorate the car for his football playoff game. As I pulled up to the attendant's station, I saw that there were a variety of car wash packages offered at different prices. The attendant, Dane, asked me which option I would prefer. I responded, "Whichever one will remove this window paint."

Dane suggested the Super Wash. I agreed, paid, and pulled my car forward onto the conveyor belt that would guide the car through the automated wash. The wash began with an employee using a scrub brush to manually tackle the obvious spots—in my case, the window paint.

Since the car was being gradually pulled forward on the conveyor belt, the employee had only a limited amount of time to remove the paint. As a result, after the car wash ended and I pulled forward into the lot, remnants of paint remained. Recall my response to Dane at the beginning of this story when he asked which wash package I wanted: "Whichever one will remove this window paint."

About this time, Dane appeared beside my driver's side window and motioned for me to pull back around for a second run through the car wash. When I arrived at the entrance, there was Dane with a bottle of degreaser and a scrub brush. He personally made sure that all of the paint was removed before my second trip through the wash.

Based on my experience at car washes, Dane's commitment to ensuring that the paint had been *completely* removed was unexpected. Ordinarily, a car wash attendant who processes hundreds of cars each day through an automated facility would treat each wash like the last one: accept payment, issue a receipt, and move on to the next vehicle—very process-focused and transactional.

But Dane chose to express genuine interest in the cleanliness of my car by following up at the end of the wash cycle to ensure that the paint had been completely removed. And when he saw that traces of the paint remained, he took steps to correct it.

Although my son's team lost its playoff game, Dane's follow-up won me over as a customer.

· · ·

Expressing genuine interest in customers embodies three truths of exceptional customer service:

1. It reflects the essence—the most critical aspect, the highest priority—of every service industry employee's job role.

2. It is always voluntary. An employee *chooses* to express genuine interest.

3. There is no additional cost. Expressing genuine interest in others is free!

Dane's job, like every employee's job, is made up of two parts: job function and job essence. When Dane advised me on car wash packages and accepted payment for the wash, he was executing job function. But when he followed up to ensure that all of the paint had been removed, he was expressing genuine interest in the cleanliness of my windows. In doing so, Dane demonstrated job essence.

Dane was compelled to advise me on wash packages. After all, knowing the difference between the packages offered is a requirement of his job—as is accepting payment. However, Dane's decisions to validate my request for paint-free windows and follow up by meeting my car at the end of the wash cycle were voluntary. He didn't have to perform these steps, and most car wash attendants don't.

How much did it cost for Dane to express genuine interest in my expectation for paint-free windows? What was the cost to follow up with me to ensure my satisfaction? How much more did Dane get paid to anticipate my need for spotless windows or pay attention to detail?

There is no additional cost to care. And while there may be incremental costs to clean a vehicle again (e.g., degreaser, soap, water, energy), these costs are negligible when compared to the long-term financial contribution of a loyal customer.

GETTING FROM ORDINARY TO EXTRAORDINARY

- Service is a verb and, as such, requires action. Action is voluntary. A service provider chooses to demonstrate initiative.
- The opposite of initiative is indifference. Often, employees are indifferent toward the needs of customers and miss opportunities to provide exceptional customer service by failing to observe their surroundings, anticipate customers' needs, or display a sense of urgency.

- To express genuine interest requires going beyond the basic customer service expectations of the job role: smiling, making eye contact, and adding a bit of energy to one's voice.

- All too often, customer greetings become transactional, and customers lose their unique identities as they dutifully conform to employees' dogmatic focus on job function (e.g., "Paper or plastic?"). Avoid using generic labels when greeting or referring to customers. Instead, use customers' names whenever possible.

- Using customers' names in circumstances other than when greeting or referring to them expresses genuine interest in them, conveys respect, and affirms their personal importance.

- Employees should approach customers, practicing assertive hospitality, rather than wait for customers to acknowledge them. This requires initiative, which may be the single most decisive attribute distinguishing exceptional customer service providers from the rest.

- The 15 × 5 Rule suggests making eye contact and smiling when you are within a distance of approximately fifteen feet of a customer, and then adding an appropriate greeting (e.g., "Good morning," "Good afternoon") when you are within approximately five feet of a customer.

- Asking questions is an effective way to express genuine interest in customers and build the rapport necessary to establish loyalty.

- Cosseting customers, which means to pamper or treat them with excessive indulgence, is a higher form of expressing genuine interest in them.

- Anticipating and fulfilling their needs without being asked to do so leads to appreciative customers.

- Remembering preferences enables service providers to express genuine interest in customers and make lasting positive impressions.

- Recall that if you do it right every time, you'll be doing it right at the right time. And by paying attention to detail, your odds of doing it right increase dramatically.

- Employees who display a sense of urgency in words and actions inspire confidence in customers.

- Solicit feedback from customers without marginalizing their suggestions or sounding defensive. When practical, implement customer feedback. Doing so validates the customer who offered the feedback when she returns and inspires more feedback in the future.

- Appropriate farewells should express genuine interest in customers and gratitude for their business. Employees must recognize that whether face-to-face, over the phone or online, a farewell is incomplete without adding, "Thank you!"

- Following up inspires customer confidence and provides assurance that they are important and their business matters.

- Expressing genuine interest reflects the essence—the most critical aspect, the highest priority—of every service industry employee's job role.

- Expressing genuine interest is always voluntary. An employee *chooses* to express genuine interest.

- There is no additional cost. Expressing genuine interest in others is free.

Applying Genuine Interest

In the space provided, record examples of how you can apply concepts from the chapter to raise customer service quality that you deliver or influence from ordinary to extraordinary!

ORDINARY	EXTRAORDINARY
Pass by customers without acknowledging them in any way.	Practice assertive hospitality by applying the 15 × 5 Rule.
•	•
•	•
•	•
•	•

3

Offer Sincere and Specific Compliments

When I ask audiences, "How many of you have received a sincere and specific compliment today?" only a smattering of hands go up. I then ask for volunteers to share the compliments they received and how they made them feel. Generally, the volunteers say the compliments made them feel appreciated, valued, respected, and important—all of which foster positive relationships. And almost always, after people share the compliments they received, their comments are validated by smiles, nods of recognition, and applause from the others in the audience.

When I question why more people in the room had not been complimented that day, I hear responses such as "People are too busy or preoccupied to notice an opportunity to compliment others," or "When people are more familiar with each other, like in a work environment or personal relationship, it's easy to take one another for granted because you see each other every day."

Over time, this lack of awareness, dulling of sensitivities, and indifference undermines the quality of the relationship—whether personal or professional. Positive relationships begin with positive interactions.

It's making the choice to express genuine interest in others as opposed to appearing indifferent toward them. We must be intentional about it by actively seeking opportunities to offer sincere and specific compliments.

Be Attentive to Opportunities to Offer Compliments

I'm not suggesting that you manufacture compliments in order to better serve your customers. Unlike expressing genuine interest, discussed in the previous chapter, the opportunity to offer a sincere and specific compliment does not present itself during every customer interaction—and insincere compliments are awkward. Just be attentive to opportunities to genuinely recognize a customer's jewelry, attire, hairstyle, or even the good behavior of her young children.

For example, you might say to a customer, "That's a great looking watch! Is it a TAG Heuer?" And then, assuming you have a genuine interest in and knowledge of watches, you can demonstrate your enthusiasm by adding something like, "Have you seen the Carrera model endorsed by Jeff Gordon?" The customer will appreciate that you recognized his watch and, if you are talking to either a watch or NASCAR enthusiast, your interaction is bound to make a positive lasting impression.

Recently, while I was in the checkout line at the supermarket, I had a chance to observe the cashier's interaction with the customer ahead of me. Typically, these encounters are transactional. For example, a screen

displays the total, the customer swipes a bank card and signs for his purchases, the cashier presents a receipt, and the customer (nine times out of ten) thanks the cashier—presumably for accepting his money. The cashier completes a set of mandatory actions that fulfill her job function. But nothing stands out. No impression is made. An opportunity to make a connection is lost forever.

However, on this particular day, the cashier noticed a bag of dog food as she scanned it (job function), and she asked, "What kind of dog do you have?" (job essence). With that, the cashier and the customer had an enthusiastic exchange about their mutual love of Labrador retrievers. It wasn't long—maybe all of twenty seconds—while the customer swiped his bank card and signed for his purchases. The cashier, by simply posing a question, had expressed genuine interest in the customer and transformed a bland and uneventful transaction into a unique and memorable experience. An impression was made. A connection was established.

The cashier's question was voluntary and reflected the essence of her job: to create a promoter. And because questions like these aren't required, we as customers don't always receive them. But when we do, they tend to leave a lasting positive impression. Perhaps when the customer returns to the store, he will quickly scan the checkout lanes to see whether or not his "friend" is working and, if so, he may go out of his way to queue in her line. The cashier may even recognize him and, recalling their previous conversation, ask about his dog.

This is how relationships form. This is how customer loyalty is earned. Customers don't establish relationships with stores—they establish relationships with the people inside the stores. Exceptional customer service is rarely the result of perfectly executed job functions that are mandated by employers. Most often, it's the result of voluntary actions such as *expressing genuine interest* (e.g., "What kind of dog do you have?") and *offering sincere and specific compliments* (e.g., "You could not have picked a breed with a better disposition") that fulfill job essence.

This example illustrates how expressing genuine interest and offering a sincere and specific compliment can occur less formally (through casual conversation) and more frequently (during routine visits to the supermarket). The same results can also be achieved through more formal and less frequent interactions, as shown in the following example.

CASE STUDY: SINCERE COMPLIMENTS
AND ATTENTION FROM A REALTOR

My wife and I have completed exactly one transaction with our realtor, Ginger Wilson, during the past thirteen years. Even so, she sends us a postcard about once a quarter to stay in touch. And she doesn't outsource the postcards to a direct mail company to blast out a quarterly marketing campaign in hopes of gaining a sale or attracting a referral. That would not be expressing genuine interest (job essence). That would be business as usual (job function).

Instead, Ginger handwrites a personalized note on the back of the postcard. These notes range from brief updates about her children or grandchildren to questions about our lives, children, and careers. And because Ginger is genuinely interested, she has chosen to subscribe to my blog. Every so often, in one of her notes, she compliments me on one of my blog posts and shares how the post enhanced the service she provides to her clients.

The effect that Ginger's handwritten notes have on me, whether or not they contain a compliment, is that I feel complimented that she values our relationship enough to take the time that's required to personalize her notes and demonstrate genuine interest in me—as a client and a friend.

Other realtors might question Ginger's use of time and money. Certainly, she has accumulated a long list of clients over the years. She must spend a considerable amount of time handwriting notes and affixing mailing labels and postage. Wouldn't it be more efficient for her to outsource the mailings to a direct mail company so that she can spend her time networking, acquiring listings, and closing sales?

So, what is the net result of Ginger's unique effort to express genuine interest in clients and offer them sincere and specific compliments? Like many of her clients, we have no plans to move, but we know whom we'll call when the time comes. In the interim, because we're promoters of Ginger, we'll continue to refer her to family and friends. To date, she has closed six transactions that have resulted from our referrals.

Apparently, other clients feel the same way. Ginger was recognized by the Denver Metro Association of Realtors as the number fifteen top producer for 2011 out of 4,500 realtors.

Factors Influencing the Offering of Compliments

So, with results like Ginger achieved, why don't all realtors express genuine interest in their clients and offer them sincere and specific compliments? Although this sounds like a rhetorical question, it bears exploring and deserves an answer. The reason most realtors utilize direct mail campaigns (job function) but do not personalize them (job essence) like Ginger is because, while direct mail campaigns are viewed as necessary to generate leads, handwritten notes are seen as optional.

The same thing happens in our personal relationships. Certain communications are required (e.g., "Did you pay the electric bill?" or "Are you planning to pick up the kids from school?"). If you choose not to have these conversations, then the lights may go off and you may get an unexpected call from your children's school. But offering sincere and specific compliments is not required. And because of that, many of us miss opportunities to offer them.

When I miss these opportunities, it's usually my wife who points them out. Perhaps I overlooked her new haircut or devalued a recent accomplishment by saying, "That's great, honey" but not asking her to elaborate on it. It's easy to become complacent in this area, and instead of communicating appreciation, you convey indifference. If you choose to focus on the routine communication that is required in a relationship while neglecting the spontaneous opportunities to appreciate the important people in your life, though the lights may remain on and the school may not call, your relationships will suffer.

Another factor that may be influencing your tendency to convey appreciation to others is your personality type. The Myers-Briggs Type Indicator (MBTI) assessment is a tool that helps people identify different aspects of their personality and clarifies their preferences. One of the dimensions, thinking/feeling, indicates a preference in how decisions are made: more detached, rational, and matching a given set of rules (thinking preference), or more empathetic, consensus-driven, and weighing the needs of the people involved (feeling preference). While people utilize both thinking and feeling functions when making decisions, they usually prefer one or the other.

When I completed the MBTI, I showed a clear preference for the thinking function. It didn't take me long to identify evidence of this in my life. For example, in my neighborhood, trash is collected on Mondays. I recall returning from a business trip on a Tuesday night and being irritated that the trash cans were still on the curb from the previous day. When I entered the house, the first thing I said to my wife was, "Why are the trash cans still on the curb?" to which she responded, "How does the house look? *[It was spotless.]* How do your kids look? *[They were bathed and in their pajamas.]* Instead of pointing out what I didn't do, why don't you appreciate what I did do?"

I later learned that those with a preference for Thinking on the MBTI tend to spontaneously critique, while those with a preference for Feeling tend to spontaneously appreciate. Whether or not you have completed an MBTI assessment, reflect on your own tendencies. Do you tend to critique more than you appreciate? If so, there may be an opportunity for you to offer a more balanced assessment of others' performance, whether at work or at home.

Author and motivational speaker Leo Buscaglia once wrote, "Too often we underestimate the power of a touch, a smile, a kind word, a listening ear, an honest compliment, or the smallest act of caring, all of which have the potential to turn a life around." You may be thinking that ". . . have the potential to turn a life around" sounds a bit dramatic. If, for example, you work in the retail industry and miss an opportunity to compliment a customer on her choice of handbags, life goes on. But consider the field of healthcare and the positive effects that compliments have on patients.

While reading the book *Love Your Patients!* by Scott Louis Diering, M.D., I came across the following passage:

> One of the nicest gifts we can give anyone is a compliment. A compliment does not cost us anything, is easy to prepare, and shows our patients that we have taken the time to recognize them as special.

For example, when someone is in pain, it is nice to recognize their tolerance. We can say, "You must be very strong to tolerate that!" Or, "You are better than I am, I would be crying!" Or, "You could give lessons on how to manage pain!" Our compliments show our admiration for their pain tolerance.

We can compliment our patients for anything, but compliments about their own healthy behaviors are always good. For example, we can compliment them on their recall for their medical history, their blood sugar log, or their initiative to come in to see us.

Further, praising our patient's healthy behaviors is a reinforcer for those behaviors. If we reinforce something, it is more likely to occur in the future. And, if we ignore their good behaviors, those good behaviors are less likely to occur again.

We all appreciate compliments. As author Robert Orben said, "A compliment is verbal sunshine." Be deliberate about recognizing opportunities to genuinely compliment others and let the sun shine bright on your relationships—and your business!

How to Offer Sincere and Specific Compliments

Up to this point, we have considered compliments to be polite expressions of praise or admiration. But it's also possible to make other people feel complimented without actually using compliments per se. We have already covered the behavior of expressing genuine interest. Three of the ways to display that behavior also double as ways for customers to feel complimented: use names, remember preferences, and solicit feedback.

Use Names

Whenever a service provider greets me by name before I've offered my name or handed her a credit card or ID, I am complimented that she valued the relationship enough to remember my name. Of course, in contrast, when I have to repeat my name again and again to a service provider on a weekly basis over the course of several months, I am equally unimpressed.

A colleague of mine works in IT consulting and had a project in Delaware that required him to commute from Denver to Dover weekly for several months. Kevin remarked to me that every time he checked into his hotel on Sunday night, the same employee would greet him with, "Have you ever stayed with us before?"

Kevin described the experience as "bizarre" and "laughable." After it happened for the third time, he began looking around for a hidden camera. Certainly, this employee was a paid actor trying to get a reaction out of him that would make for good reality television. Sadly, there were no cameras. There was only a disengaged employee who was going through the motions, performing his job functions while treating each guest just like the last guest.

Even if you don't remember a customer's name, you can show that you remember her by recognizing her face. Contrast Kevin's experience with the reception that another colleague, Shawn, received upon arrival at the Edmonton Marriott at River Cree Resort in Alberta, Canada. I received a voice mail from Shawn shortly after he checked in at the hotel. A portion of his message follows.

CASE STUDY: RECOGNITION FROM A HOTEL DESK CLERK

I walked in the front door of the Edmonton Marriott and the desk clerk, named Rizwan, looked at me and said, "Welcome back, sir. It's good to see you."

I said to him, "You know, a little thing like that is just amazing to me given the hundreds—or even thousands—of people you see at this hotel."

I haven't been here in around two months, but it just makes it so nice. And it's funny because next week I come back here [to Edmonton] and I haven't booked my hotel yet, and that just solidified it. I said to him, "I'll be staying with you again next week."

That one little thing—just the gesture of remembering my face—was genuinely impressive to me. This was a great case where, guess what, they just got my business for another trip—in reality, for several trips in the future. And they're not even the cheapest, by the way. It would be significantly cheaper at some other hotels. It's just that important.

Even though Rizwan did not recall Shawn's name, the fact that he simply recognized him was enough to trigger Shawn's enthusiastic reaction, create a lasting positive impression, and solidify his status as a promoter of the Edmonton Marriott at River Cree Resort.

Remember Preferences

My wife and I recently hosted Reid, a friend's son, who moved to Colorado from Texas to play in a summer collegiate baseball league. Knowing he was going to be staying with us for several weeks, I discreetly asked his mother for some of his preferences pertaining to cereals, snacks, and beverages.

Armed with Reid's preferences, we stocked up on all of his favorites. When he checked the cupboard, there was a box of Cheerios. When he was looking for a snack, there just happened to be a box of Nilla Wafers. When he had a sweet tooth, low and behold, there was a package of Twizzlers. And when he was thirsty, he found plenty of Coca-Cola. Because I valued the relationship, I made the effort to learn Reid's preferences. Remember that service is a verb and, as such, requires action.

The opposite of valuing the relationship is taking the relationship for granted. Instead of appearing interested and making a positive lasting impression, you appear indifferent and make no impression at all.

The same is true for customers. Whenever you remember their preferences, whether it's their daily coffee order or their biannual tailoring details, they feel complimented that you value the relationship enough to do so.

Shortly after Reid moved back home to Texas, we discovered that he had inadvertently left behind a pair of practice pants. When we packed them up to return them, we included drawings from the kids (who missed him terribly) and, of course, a package of Twizzlers.

Solicit Feedback

By asking customers for feedback, preferably face-to-face or over the phone, and then acting on it, it's possible to reinforce their importance and validate their unique insight into your business.

Too often, the act of soliciting feedback is reduced to an obligatory, process-focused exercise that produces customers' comments and suggestions that then seemingly fall into a black hole. Like many consumers, I mostly toss the satisfaction surveys I receive because of the memories of providing thoughtful feedback without ever being acknowledged.

Think about it. When is the last time you received a letter, a phone call, or an e-mail pertaining to feedback that you provided to a company? If you can think of one, chances are you were surprised to hear back, and likely, a positive lasting impression was made. Do you want to know why many businesses solicit feedback but few respond to feedback? Here's why: In most companies, soliciting customer feedback has been formalized. It's someone's job function. There's a process for it. It's mandatory.

Businesses have to ask you and me for feedback. It's a *required* element of their customer-centric strategy that they can execute, quantify, and publicize. But the decision to respond to customers or act on their feedback is *voluntary*. Businesses don't have to do it, and most don't.

There's a story about Stew Leonard, Sr., founder of the renowned Stew Leonard's supermarkets, that illustrates the importance of soliciting customer feedback and then acting on it.

One day, Leonard received a written customer suggestion that his store should sell fresh fish. At the time, the store did sell fresh fish. They sent a van to Boston each morning to buy fresh fish, returned to the store in Westport, Connecticut, prepared and sealed the fish in plastic wrap on Styrofoam trays, and displayed the packages on ice for shoppers' perusal. Leonard could have easily dismissed the suggestion but instead honored the feedback by calling the customer to inquire further about what she meant.

During that call, he learned that the customer defined fresh fish as being laid loose on ice rather than sealed in plastic wrap on a Styrofoam tray. He thanked the customer for her suggestion and decided to conduct a little experiment at the store. The next day, he instructed the seafood department to display half the fresh fish wrapped in plastic as usual and the other half laid loose on ice. One week into the experiment, he found that the fish that had been laid loose on ice outsold the fish wrapped in plastic by a margin of three to one and that his gross sales of fresh fish had doubled!

By soliciting feedback and then acting on it, Leonard complimented the customer and reinforced her personal importance. Imagine how she must have felt when she returned to the seafood department and realized that her suggestion had been implemented. How would you have felt?

And Don't Be Afraid to Be Unconventional

When customers feel complimented, they feel important. Personal importance refers to one's importance as a customer and the value she brings to the business through referrals, repeat purchases, and other benefits of loyalty. Using names, remembering preferences, and soliciting feedback are all conventional ways to compliment customers by reinforcing their importance. But some of the most memorable ways—as modeled by realtor Ginger Wilson (discussed earlier in this chapter)— are the least conventional.

Years ago, the executive team of a Marriott hotel in Denver was making a sales presentation to a group of executives from United Airlines. Marriott was competing with a number of local hotels for a significant number of airline crew room nights for the upcoming year.

While the hotel's director of sales and general manager were making their pitch from the front of the boardroom, a cell phone began to ring from the inside pocket of the general manager's suit jacket. At first, he seemed to ignore the call and continued his presentation. When it was clear that the phone was distracting the group's attention, he paused, reached inside his pocket, and removed the phone.

His executive team sat mortified. Not only had he forgotten to turn off his phone, but he was actually going to accept a call in the middle of a crucial sales presentation, to the dismay of the United Airlines executives.

It was at that moment that the general manager answered his phone, looked at the senior United Airlines executive, and, with a wry smile, said, "Excuse me sir. I have Bill Marriott on the phone. He'd like to personally ask for your business."

Again, put yourself in the customer's shoes. Would you have felt complimented by this gesture? Would you have felt important? Evidently, it made an impression on the executive. Marriott was awarded the contract.

Recognize Coworkers

Up to now, we've seen examples of compliments as they pertain to our "customers" at work and at home. While our customers at work are commonly thought of as consumers of products and services, for the remainder of this chapter, I'd like to focus on our *internal* customers at work: our coworkers. There's a saying that "happy employees make happy customers." It's true. Employees are more satisfied when their contributions are recognized by their immediate supervisors. And because employees tend to duplicate behaviors they have seen praised, customers benefit as the recipients of greater consistency in product and service quality.

A key finding of a ten-year, 200,000-person study by the Jackson Organization (now HealthStream Research), is that the central characteristic of truly effective management—the element that shows up time and again in every great workplace—is a manager's ability to recognize employees' talents and contributions in a *purposeful* manner.

I once worked with Phil, a department head who confessed to me that he frequently missed opportunities to compliment others. As a result, he appeared indifferent toward the exceptional quality of work being performed around him. This perception was confirmed by the results of an employee opinion survey that rated his employees' responses to a question about whether or not their contributions at work were recognized.

Phil told me that while he really did appreciate employees' contributions at work, he often was too preoccupied with meetings, his to-do list, and other priorities to take notice. He resolved to be more intentional about affirming the contributions of his coworkers. To accomplish this, he used a system that I refer to as Five Coin Recognition.

Here is how it works. At the start of each day, Phil would put five coins in his right pocket. Each time he stopped to recognize an employee, he would shift one of the coins over to his left pocket (at some point after the interaction). The coins served as physical reminders for him to pause throughout the day to compliment the work of others.

If this seems rigid or calculated to you, understand that the quality of execution (of this or any other performance management technique) is determined by one's motive. If Phil's motive was solely to increase his department's employee opinion survey ratings in order to appear more effective as a manager, then his actions would likely be perceived as rehearsed and insincere. But because he was motivated by a genuine desire to recognize others, this system was an effective one.

At the end of the day, all Phil had to do was count the number of coins in his left pocket. If there were only one or two coins, then he realized that he had been too preoccupied that day to recognize employees. But if there were four or five coins in his left pocket, then he knew he had done a better job of recognizing employees by offering sincere and specific compliments.

Here's another creative way to offer sincere and specific compliments in a purposeful manner. Figure 3-1 depicts a free compliment poster. What I love about this poster is that it serves as a physical reminder to recognize others. And because it's right in front of us, it helps us to be

FIGURE 3-1 Free compliment poster.

deliberate about offering compliments in situations where we otherwise would not—for no other reason than it simply did not occur to us.

Consider creating your own free compliments poster with compliments that are tailored to your work environment. This will encourage employees to tear off compliments and share them with coworkers. Whether or not there is an appropriate preprinted compliment to fit the situation, the very act of displaying such a poster gets employees talking and raises awareness about offering sincere and specific compliments in the workplace.

According to Gallup, 65 percent of North Americans report that they weren't recognized at work during the previous year. This underscores the need for managers to be intentional about demonstrating appreciation and deliberate in the way they recognize employees' talents and contributions.

When I received my first management position with Marriott in 1992, I worked for a general manager named Mark Conklin. Although Mark oversaw more than 200 employees, each employee received a handwritten birthday card from him in the mail. And he didn't merely scrawl his signature beneath a generic, preprinted "Happy Birthday!" message. He took the time to write a full paragraph that highlighted a recent contribution the employee had made to the hotel, thanked him for his commitment to excellence, and wished him a happy birthday.

It would have been easier for Mark to distribute the cards through interoffice mail so that employees received their cards at work, but he chose to mail the cards to their homes. He reasoned that the cards would be opened in front of family members and that employees could take pride in sharing the positive comments about their valuable contributions at work.

Although this was twenty years ago, I still have the handwritten notes I received from Mark on my birthday. I keep them with the memorabilia I collected during my twenty years with the company. That's how much they meant to me.

On December 13, 2011, J. W. Marriott, Jr. (known familiarly as Bill) announced that he was stepping down as chief executive officer of Marriott International. Arne Sorenson, the chief operating officer, assumed the CEO role in March 2012. Sorenson is only the third CEO in the company's eighty-five–year history and the first from outside the Marriott family.

The stability of having J. W. Marriott in the CEO role for nearly forty years had provided Wall Street analysts with a level of confidence—even during some tumultuous economic cycles. His presence had also assured the company's quarter-million employees that they would be treated fairly and with respect. Customers even took comfort in knowing that there was a real "Mr. Marriott" standing behind the Marriott brand.

Since Sorenson assumed the CEO role, there was no longer a Marriott in the top job. Thus, there was likely to be a bit more scrutiny by Wall Street. In addition, employees might be more skeptical of corporate initiatives, and customers might question the company's long-standing commitment to maintaining the high standards of product and service quality championed by the founder's son.

About the time the announcement was made, I was in the process of sending holiday cards and decided to send Sorenson a card with a brief note congratulating him on his promotion. Although I had worked for Marriott for many years, I did not know Sorenson personally. In fact, I had never even met him. My only connection to him is that I used to work for Marriott. I certainly never expected to hear back from him. To my surprise, the soon-to-be CEO of a $25-billion company took the time to send me a handwritten note thanking me for my card.

3 January 2012

Dear Steve —
Thanks for your note of congratulations. It's always great to hear from our alums.
We're all going to miss Mr. Marriott, but fortunately we'll have him around to keep us on our toes a bit longer.
Happy New Year,
Arne Sorenson

After reading Sorenson's note, I was reminded of the birthday cards I received from Mark Conklin twenty years ago—and I was reassured that Marriott was in very good hands.

When research firm Watson Wyatt asked employees to identify "very significant" motivators of performance, 66 percent said "appreciation." By recognizing employees' talents and contributions in a *purposeful* manner, appreciation is not left to chance or unwittingly sacrificed because of the demands of a busy schedule.

. . .

As demonstrated throughout this chapter, offering sincere and specific compliments to others embodies three truths of exceptional customer service:

1. It reflects the essence—the most critical aspect, the highest priority—of every service industry employee's job role.
2. It is always voluntary. An employee *chooses* to offer sincere and specific compliments.
3. There is no additional cost. Compliments are free.

Consider the job role of my former general manager, Mark Conklin. Like every general manager's job, it is made up of two parts: job function and job essence. Most large companies have a system in place to formally recognize employee milestones, such as employment anniversaries and birthdays, but even recognition can be reduced to job function if done in a way that feels automated, mechanical, or impersonal.

Whenever I receive an unsigned card with a preprinted message or a card that is signed with an electronic signature, it reeks of efficiency and reduces the effectiveness of the gesture. So, while the act of utilizing systems to recognize employee milestones is a manager's job function, by taking the time to write a personalized note offering a sincere and specific compliment, Mark demonstrated job essence.

Managers at large companies are often *required* to recognize employee milestones. It's all part of a balanced scorecard approach to management that holds managers accountable to a variety of metrics, including employee satisfaction. However, Mark's decisions to handwrite personalized notes that recognized recent contributions made by employees, and to mail the cards to employees' homes so that they would be opened in front of family members, were *voluntary* decisions. He didn't have to take these extra steps, and most general managers don't.

How much did it cost for Mark to offer sincere and specific compliments by handwriting notes and mailing the cards to employees' homes? Remember: *There is no additional cost to care.* While Mark no doubt set aside time in his schedule to record personalized notes in the cards and incurred postage expenses that could have been spared by distributing the cards through interoffice mail, these costs are negligible when compared to the long-term financial contribution of an engaged workforce.

According to Frederick Reichheld, author of *The Loyalty Effect*, just a 5 percent increase in employee loyalty can increase profits by as much as 50 percent. This reinforces the positive correlation between employee satisfaction and business results.

One of Bill Marriott's "Twelve Rules of Success" is: "Take good care of your employees, and they'll take good care of your customers, and the customers will come back." Taking care of the important people in your life, at work and at home, begins by appreciating them. One way to accomplish this is to be purposeful about offering sincere and specific compliments.

GETTING FROM ORDINARY TO EXTRAORDINARY

- Positive relationships begin with positive interactions. We must be intentional about actively seeking opportunities to offer sincere and specific compliments.
- Employees are paid to execute a required set of job functions. But the employee's choice to offer a sincere and specific compliment, which costs nothing, is voluntary.
- Customers don't establish relationships with businesses. They establish relationships with the people inside the businesses.
- If you choose to focus on the routine communication that is required in a relationship while neglecting the spontaneous opportunities to appreciate the important people in your life, your relationships will suffer.

- People with a Myers-Briggs Type Indicator (MBTI) preference for Thinking tend to spontaneously critique, while those with a preference for Feeling tend to spontaneously appreciate. Reflect on your own tendencies. Do you tend to critique more than you appreciate? If so, there may be an opportunity for you to offer a more balanced assessment of others' performance, whether at work or at home.
- It's possible to compliment others without using compliments per se. For instance, customers *feel complimented* when service providers recognize them by using their names, remembering their preferences, and soliciting their feedback.
- A key finding of the 200,000-person study by the Jackson Group is that the central characteristic of truly effective management is a manager's ability to recognize employees' talents and contributions in a *purposeful* manner.
- Offering sincere and specific compliments reflects the essence—the most critical aspect, the highest priority—of every service industry employee's job role.
- Offering sincere and specific compliments is always voluntary. An employee *chooses* to offer sincere and specific compliments.
- There is no additional cost to offer sincere and specific compliments. Compliments are free.

Applying Sincere and Specific Compliments

In the space provided, record examples of how you can apply concepts from the chapter to raise customer service quality that you deliver or influence from ordinary to extraordinary!

ORDINARY	EXTRAORDINARY
Automate direct mail campaigns in order to efficiently remain in contact with clientele.	Personalize direct mailings with handwritten notes in order to foster authentic relationships with clientele.
•	•
•	•
•	•
•	•

4

Share Unique Knowledge

This chapter is dedicated to a dear friend and colleague named John Barclay who passed away in the spring of 2007. A former high school teacher who held a master's degree from Boston College, John was a champion of knowledge. At the same time, early in his career, he studied and performed as an actor in England and continued to direct community theater productions through 2006. John's unique background of education and theater made him an irresistible national trainer at Marriott International.

Having worked with John presenting training classes, I came to appreciate his remarkable ability to captivate adult learners with his energetic approach to the training manual's content. Aside from his public speaking skills, John also had a knack for sharing relevant, interesting stories that reinforced important lessons from the text. One evening, John and I were giving each other feedback, and I shared this observation with him. The conversation that followed introduced me to the concept of unique knowledge.

Knowing I had worked at a hotel in New York City for nearly four years, John asked, "Steve, what are some of the names of the meeting rooms at your former hotel?"

I responded, "Odets, Wilder, Cantor, Jolson. . . ."

"If I were a customer and asked you why the meeting room was named Odets," he interrupted, "what would you say?"

I thought about it for a moment and realized that I didn't know the significance of the proper name *Odets*. I admitted this to John saying, "You know, I just got so used to the name representing a meeting room that I never really gave it much thought."

John didn't lecture me, but he made the point that it's our responsibility to know the significance of proper names, to learn the backgrounds of key people, and to uncover the histories and stories attributed to the neighborhoods and buildings in which we work.

Reflecting on this conversation, I had learned a valuable lesson that evening: Job knowledge is sufficient to meet expectations and satisfy customers, but unique knowledge is required if your goal is to exceed expectations and delight customers.

Unique Knowledge Brings More Value to the Customer Experience

The subject of job knowledge was introduced in Chapter 1 during the discussion of job function and job essence. Job knowledge informs employees so that they can execute their job functions accurately, safely, and efficiently. Job knowledge (e.g., hours of operation, product specifications, return policy) is required of employees and expected by customers. Job knowledge resides in training programs and policy and procedure manuals. Employees are paid to acquire job knowledge and share it with customers and coworkers.

Unique knowledge, however, enables employees to reflect job essence, their highest priority at work. It is not required of employees and is not expected by customers. Unique knowledge goes beyond that which is typically associated with a job role. It has character and substance. Most often, it is not found in a book or manual. Employees voluntarily acquire unique knowledge and share it with customers and coworkers.

Unique knowledge, when shared with customers, can mean the difference between a predictable transaction and a refreshing service experience. Here are a few examples of how this knowledge might be used by a customer-facing employee:

- **Unique knowledge about the building.** "There's quite a bit a history in this hotel. In fact, in 1926, the famed magician Harry Houdini escaped from a sealed underwater coffin beneath this very roof when it was the Shelton Towers Hotel."

- **Unique knowledge about the neighborhood.** "Our restaurant is located in the Gaslamp Quarter, which is named after the gas lamps that lined the streets in the early 1900s when the area was a red-light district known as Stingaree. The name was probably derived from the fierce stingray fish in the San Diego Bay. It was said that you could be stung as badly in the Stingaree as in the bay!"

- **Unique knowledge about the staff.** "Our head tennis pro is a former ATP Tour player who competed against former world-class players like Andre Agassi, Jim Courier, and Pete Sampras. Would you like to schedule an hour lesson with him?"

- **Unique knowledge about the product.** "Here's your espresso macchiato. Did you know that *macchiato* means 'marked' or 'stained' in Italian? The espresso is 'marked' with a teaspoon of milk."

- **Unique knowledge about proper names.** "Your meeting is being held in the Odets meeting room on the fourth floor. The room is named after the playwright Clifford Odets, who wrote the plays *Waiting for Lefty* and *Awake and Sing*. Several of our meeting rooms are named after other well-known playwrights. After all, you are in the Theater District!"

While customers appreciate nice employees, they value knowledgeable employees. And the more unique knowledge that employees possess, the more value they bring to the customer experience.

The Benefits of Unique Knowledge

Unique knowledge, like job knowledge, is beneficial for employees to possess, but for different reasons. Job knowledge informs, supports sales, and provides a common broad perspective about a company's products and services. Unique knowledge is captivating, creates sales, and provides an exclusive "insider's" perspective into a company's products and services.

Unique Knowledge Captivates

Whereas job knowledge informs, unique knowledge captivates. As customers, we are interested in gaining unique knowledge from others. When exposed to unique knowledge, we tend to concentrate and listen intently.

Radio disc jockeys are masters at revealing unique knowledge to their listeners deliberately and in stages. They recognize that it can be entrancing and, when done well, has the power to charm audiences into listening to seven minutes worth of commercials between songs.

I recently heard a local DJ share this illustration of unique knowledge: "There was one Pink Floyd song in which the lead vocalist was not a member of the band. And I'll play that song next." I then waited through several minutes of commercials before he returned to finish the story: "You won't hear the vocals of Roger Waters or David Gilmour in this Pink Floyd song. Due to a relentless recording schedule, Waters's voice was shot and Gilmour didn't want to sing the song. So they asked a friend who was recording in a studio down the hall to help them out. Here's Pink Floyd's 'Have a Cigar' with lead singer, Roy Harper."

Radio ad sponsors also love it when DJs share unique knowledge in this way because it motivates listeners to stay tuned to the station during commercial breaks rather than switching stations to avoid hearing commercials.

It's also possible to captivate customers with unique knowledge in a customer service setting. I recall a flight attendant using unique knowledge to mitigate the effects of a delay at

Chicago's O'Hare International Airport. As we sat on the tarmac awaiting a gate assignment after landing, he used the plane's intercom system to share interesting facts about the airport.

"The airport was originally constructed in 1942–43," he began from memory, "as a manufacturing plant for Douglas C-54s during World War II. After the war, when it became an airport, it was named Orchard Field Airport after Orchard Place, a nearby farming community that produced apples and other crops. This was the origin of O'Hare's airport code: ORD."

As interested passengers listened, he continued, "The airport was renamed O'Hare International Airport in 1949 after Edward O'Hare, the U.S. Navy's first flying ace and Medal of Honor recipient in World War II."

As the plane suddenly pulled forward in the direction of the gates, he said, "It appears a gate has become available. I hope you enjoyed learning a little bit about O'Hare's history. Welcome to Chicago!"

At that moment, the cabin erupted in spontaneous applause.

Unique Knowledge Creates Sales

Whereas job knowledge supports sales, unique knowledge creates sales. Consider the job knowledge that is expected from a typical waiter at a fine restaurant. For instance, he might be expected to know the menu items well in terms of their origin, preparation, and ingredients. The waiter would also be expected to know about aspects of the menu that might change from time to time, such as the market prices of fresh fish, daily specials, and the soup de jour.

Unlike job knowledge, unique knowledge is unexpected. It is refreshing, interesting, and perhaps even entertaining. Because it's unique, it adds to the service experience. Unique knowledge is special and more likely to make a lasting positive impression on customers. It even has the power to influence sales.

Let's take, for example, two waiters introducing the same item to a customer: one waiter relating job knowledge (expected and routine) and the other conveying unique knowledge (unexpected and refreshing):

Job knowledge: "Tonight, our featured appetizer is the pâté de foie gras. May I interest you in an order?"

Unique knowledge: "Our chef trained at the prestigious Restaurant School in Philadelphia and apprenticed at Le Bec Fin. She also traveled to France to refine her knowledge of French delicacies such as truffles, escargot, and foie gras. In fact, pâté de foie gras is our featured appetizer. May I tempt you with an order?"

Now, seriously, if you're on the receiving end of each of these proposals, which one might you accept—even if you previously had no intention of ordering an appetizer? Exactly.

And here's something else I've found to be true: Which proposal is likely to bring up the question of price, which may influence a customer's decision of whether or not to order the appetizer? After listening to the second proposal (and salivating, as the waiter's delivery has likely activated a Pavlovian response), I would expect that, for most customers, the price of the appetizer would be irrelevant.

So, make it a point to acquire as much unique knowledge as possible about products, services, the culture and history of your business, the building and neighborhood you operate in, the people in the organization, and even proper names (e.g., "Why is the steakhouse chain named Ruth's Chris, anyway?"). You provide your customers with a richer service experience and they will make you . . . well, richer!

Here's another example involving meat cutters at today's sprawling supermarkets. As a child, I recall the neighborhood butcher on Hillside Avenue in Hartford, Connecticut, sharing unique knowledge with my grandmother about different cuts of meat, preparation techniques, and tips for using leftovers. Because of the rapport he built with his customers by sharing his expertise, he had license to make suggestions and even cross-sell other products such as dry rubs and marinades.

As the scale of operations has grown at most supermarkets, many meat cutters have disappeared from out front to the back, where interactions with shoppers are limited to announcements over the intercom. The roles of these expert food preparers shifted from that of a familiar, customer-focused butcher who formed close bonds with shoppers, remembered their names and preferences, answered their questions, and offered suggestions, to an anonymous, process-focused worker whose priority is churning out enough hamburger, chicken breasts, sausage links, and fish fillets to fill the meat and seafood cases.

In my experience, butchers are an untapped resource in most supermarkets. Rather than being positioned as professional food preparers (or even chefs) with unique knowledge to share, they are often marginalized as simple meat cutters who, if you can find one, might be able to, say, cut your tenderloin into two-inch fillets. The difference separates a memorable, customer-focused experience from an ordinary, process-focused transaction at the meat or seafood counter.

For years, the meat cutters and fishmongers at my local supermarket limited their preparation advice to suggestions like "just trim the fat and add some salt and pepper" (job knowledge). Instead, they could be offering tips like, for grilled salmon, suggesting that customers marinate the fillets in equal parts honey, soy sauce, butter, olive oil, and brown sugar, and garnish with a lemon wedge and parsley. Further, if they were interested, they could provide grilling advice such as telling you to coat the grilling surface with olive oil to prevent sticking, preheat the grill to 325 degrees, be sure to grill the fillets skin side first, and target an internal temperature of 140 degrees (unique knowledge).

Think about the first suggestion above—trimming the fat and adding salt and pepper. By just offering job knowledge, the only two ingredients the butcher mentioned were salt and pepper. I'll go out on a limb and predict that most supermarket customers have these seasonings in their homes. Now consider the second suggestion—marinating in honey, soy sauce, butter, olive oil, and brown sugar, and garnishing with lemon and parsley. By offering unique knowledge, the butcher has mentioned seven ingredients. If customers' interest has been piqued, what are the chances that most of them are confident that they have all seven ingredients at home?

If it's me, after running through a mental checklist of the pantry, I'm picking up honey, brown sugar, lemons, and parsley. Think about your own situation. What would you be adding to your list? The point is that by sharing unique knowledge, the butcher expresses genuine interest in his customer, conveys his authentic enthusiasm for his craft, makes a positive lasting impression on the customer, and increases sales for the supermarket!

While unique knowledge is most often conveyed orally, it can also be conveyed in written form through signage. I recall waiting in line at Starbucks and noticing a display of coffee mugs that were selling for $8.95. My first thought was that the last thing I needed was another coffee mug. And, if I was going to buy one, I likely wouldn't pay full price. I'd look around for a mug with a bright red price sticker on it because, after all, a mug's a mug, right? Maybe not.

Alongside the mugs, I noticed a conspicuous display card containing a bit of background information on the mug that read:

SAFARA MUG: MADE BY POTTERS IN TOKI CITY, JAPAN, USING TECHNIQUES PASSED FROM GENERATION TO GENERATION FOR MORE THAN 400 YEARS. $8.95

No longer was this "just another coffee mug." It was a unique piece of pottery that had been crafted by artisans with specialized knowledge that had been passed down from one generation to the next. And no longer was a selling price of $8.95 too high. It appeared reasonable, given the origin and craftsmanship of the mug.

Now, I have no illusions that this mug will appreciate in value and one day become a collector's item worthy of being displayed in a case at the Smithsonian. The point is that this commodity, a coffee mug, had been transformed into a piece of art simply by the sharing of unique knowledge.

Unique knowledge adds value to the customer experience. It's interesting and compelling in the sense that it attracts attention. You notice it. It's memorable.

Consider your own products and services. How can you add value by sharing unique knowledge? What story might you tell that captivates your customers, repositions your offerings as exclusive, and justifies your price premiums?

Unique Knowledge Provides an "Insider's" Perspective

Whereas job knowledge provides a common broad perspective about a company's products and services, unique knowledge offers an exclusive "insider's" perspective into a company's products and services. By offering privileged, insider information to customers, you are sharing unique knowledge. Examples include ways to avoid long lines at Disney World, how to nab theater tickets for half-price, how to find a nearby jogging trail offering spectacular views, or locating that independent Italian restaurant preferred by locals.

Eldon Larson, owner of Wine Experience Café in Aurora, Colorado, offers insider information that demystifies the wine ordering experience, enabling servers to confidently offer wine suggestions to their guests. According to Larson:

> It's not uncommon for servers who are new to fine dining to have limited experience with wine and to be intimidated by the many varietals and guidelines for offering food and wine pairing suggestions. Being that the varietals' origins are in France, I use a map of the country to introduce less experienced staff to the regions that produce these wines. From there, I make connections to other countries that produce wine using similar grapes. And by offering tastes of varietals from different countries, servers can note these distinctions in their tasting notes.

Larson also proposes a map-based system to support less experienced staff in assisting their guests with wine selections while providing unique knowledge about wine varietals. Regardless of whether you are the waiter taking the order or the guest placing it, you can benefit from Larson's approach.

Throughout their exposure to the wines, trainees are encouraged to put into words what they are nosing and tasting. This helps them to articulate to restaurant guests the difference between a dry French Riesling and a sweet German Riesling or an airy French Pinot Noir and a darker, richer Oregon Pinot Noir.

While Larson's formal wine training takes about ninety days for servers to complete, by using a simple map of France depicting each of its wine regions, from the start they are equipped to make informed wine recommendations that aid in getting wine on the table. And by sharing insights from Larson's map-based system with restaurant guests as a "peek behind the curtain," servers have the potential to impart unique knowledge and leave a lasting positive impression.

How to Share Unique Knowledge

Similar to job knowledge, there are different types of unique knowledge including knowledge that pertains to the product or service, the competition, or the customer. But unlike job knowledge that is expected of the employee, the absence of which may lead to customer disappointment, unique knowledge is often unexpected, and its presence may lead to customer delight—and a sale!

Share Knowledge About the Product or Service

A couple of years ago, I was shopping for a garment bag for my wife. Her job required travel, and her current bag was showing serious signs of wear and tear. I stopped into one of those mall luggage stores, and the salesperson showed me a black Tumi garment bag.

As I was inspecting the bag, I noticed that the price was $400. I said to the salesperson, "Wow. I really like the bag, but $400 is more than I was planning to spend. Do these bags ever go on sale?"

"The only time I've seen these bags discounted is when a color or style has been discontinued," she answered.

I didn't see anything else I was interested in buying at the store, so I thanked the salesperson and left.

A few minutes later, I stopped by a second luggage store at the mall and looked around. Again, the only garment bag that caught my eye was the same black Tumi bag. I checked the price tag: $400. A salesperson approached and asked if she could answer any questions. I posed the same question I'd asked in the previous store, saying, "I really like this bag, but $400 is more than I was planning to spend. Do these bags ever go on sale?"

Again, the salesperson answered, "These bags are only discounted when a color or style has been discontinued." I thought to myself,

"Well, at least they're consistent." But then the salesperson said something I hadn't heard before.

"You're right," she said. "This luggage is not cheap, and $400 is quite an investment in a garment bag. However, were you aware of Tumi's unique product warranty and Tracer® recovery system?"

My quizzical expression prompted her to continue. She said:

"This bag is made out of ballistic nylon and can withstand the wear associated with frequent travel. With limited exceptions, if your Tumi product is damaged during the first twelve months you own it—including damage caused by wear and tear, airlines, or other transit damage—Tumi will cover all repair expenses, including shipping costs to and from its repair facility. And if they determine that the product is damaged beyond repair, they will replace it. And Tumi's warranty extends from the second through the fifth year of ownership covering any repairs due to defective materials or workmanship, including any structural defects."

By this time, I was nodding in approval (a buying signal that didn't go unnoticed by the salesperson). She continued:

"Also, Tumi offers an exclusive, complimentary program called the Tumi Tracer® Product Recovery Program that helps reunite its customers with their lost or stolen luggage. Each bag contains an individual product number printed on a special metal plate that is permanently affixed to the product. When registered, that number, along with the owner's contact information, is entered into the Tracer® database. Since its introduction in 1999, Tumi Tracer® has helped thousands of its customers reclaim their valuable Tumi products."

I bought the $400 garment bag I hadn't even considered purchasing just fifteen minutes earlier at the first luggage store—and all because the salesperson took the time to share her unique knowledge and convince me that, due to my wife's frequent travel, I really could not afford *not* to buy this bag!

You might be thinking, "Doesn't all of this information about product warranty and features constitute job knowledge?" And you'd be half-right because about half of the knowledge shared by the salesperson was expected. But when an employee's job knowledge exceeds that which might reasonably be expected by the consumer, then it becomes unique knowledge.

Share Knowledge About the Competition

Providing job knowledge about a competitor's product or service is expected and may assist a customer in making an informed buying decision. But sharing unique knowledge about a competitor's product or service is often unanticipated and may influence a customer to make the *right* buying decision.

Professional salespeople recognize that, in addition to obtaining knowledge about the specifications, features, and benefits of the products they sell, they must also learn as much as they can about the products offered by the competition.

Perhaps this behavior was best modeled by Kris Kringle in the 1947 movie *Miracle on 34th Street*. While serving as the Macy's department store Santa, he caused quite a stir by directing holiday shoppers to Gimbels and other stores to find the exact toys they were looking for. He was able to do this because of his unique knowledge about the toy selection at competing retailers (or, perhaps, he really was Santa Claus?).

What I appreciate about this example is that, in addition to illustrating unique knowledge, it also demonstrates an attitude of abundance that carried over to store management. Rather than feeling threatened by the competition and treating them like the enemy, management embraced the competition and treated them as partners. As a result, Macy's better served its customers while improving overall industry sales. A rising tide lifts all boats.

But Hollywood isn't the only place this attitude of abundance exists. Here's an example about by my father-in-law, Ed, who is a restaurateur in Denver.

CASE STUDY: A RESTAURATEUR EMBRACES THE COMPETITION

Several years ago, Ed took out an expensive full-page ad in the local newspaper that read, "Take this ad to your favorite restaurant and receive $10 off dinner for two." The ad did not specify the name of a restaurant or provide any contact information.

Diners then began to show up at restaurants throughout the Denver area with the coupon, and puzzled restaurateurs contacted the paper to see who took out the ad. As the word spread among restaurateurs that my father-in-law was responsible for the ad, they began to call him at his restaurant.

The conversations went something like this: "Hey Ed, there are some customers here at my restaurant who are trying to use *your* coupon!" to which my father-in-law responded, "It's not my coupon. It's everyone's coupon. But if you don't wish to be their favorite restaurant, then send them to me. I would be honored to be considered their favorite restaurant!"

Over the years, Ed's attitude of abundance lowered the barriers among competitors. As a former National Restaurant Association board member and established leader within the Colorado Restaurant Association, he worked hard to pass reforms that would benefit the entire industry. He also frequented many competitors' restaurants, bringing guests, to support them while acquiring unique knowledge about their wine lists, menu offerings, prices, and other competitive factors, in order to better serve his own customers.

Ed's attitude was infectious. On one occasion, a group of us were enjoying predinner drinks on the patio of one of Ed's restaurants. Our group included a competing restaurateur, Wayne, who owned a local steakhouse. After several of us had expressed an interest in ordering steaks for dinner, Ed said, "I know where we can get the best steaks in town!"

Although his own restaurant's menu listed several steak entrees, Ed called Wayne's steakhouse and placed an order for four complete steak entrees, arranged for their delivery to the patio of his restaurant, and covered all the costs.

Contrast Ed's approach with the typical posture toward competitors of arrogance (e.g., "Our steaks are better than their steaks") and suspicion (e.g., "I bet he's really here to recruit my employees"). This attitude is often cultivated by an underlying belief that there is only so much reward (e.g., market share, profit, talent) to go around, and if competitors are rewarded in some way, then I am irrevocably harmed by their success.

Practicing humility, candor, and graciousness toward competitors creates an environment of openness and trust. There is a willingness, even an enthusiasm, to share unique knowledge (best practices, not trade secrets) with the goal of improving the product and service quality offered to customers.

Share Knowledge About the Customer

Customers expect you to have job knowledge about their habits, preferences, or demographics, and such knowledge may assist employees in better understanding customers and meeting their expectations. But having unique knowledge about their habits, preferences, or demographics is often not expected by customers and may enable employees to more fully understand them in order to *exceed* their expectations.

Earlier, I suggested that capturing and archiving customers' preferences expressed genuine interest in customers. It also compliments them by reinforcing their personal importance as customers. Whenever a company collects a customer's preferences, it has acquired unique knowledge about that individual. This information is now at the company's disposal and may be the difference between meeting and exceeding the customer's expectations in the future.

Airlines, hotels, and car rental companies have maintained these databases for years in order to anticipate the needs of their repeat customers. Generally, a customer's preference for an aisle seat, a nonsmoking room with a king-size bed, or a full-size automobile won't change from month to month. When businesses archive these preferences in customer profiles, it saves their clients time when making reservations and affirms that they are recognized by the brand as repeat customers.

My local supermarket offers a customer retention program. (Although they call it a loyalty program, it's really a retention program because customers are motivated by discounts to participate.) After enrolling, customers receive a discount card that is input during checkout. In this way, unique knowledge about each member's preferences are captured and stored following each transaction.

Over time, the supermarket gains powerful insights into customers' shopping patterns, preferred brands, and total spending. It becomes a cinch to tailor marketing promotions to each customer's household based on the unique knowledge obtained.

But there are other ways to capture unique knowledge about customers. Social media, for example, provides a real-time resource for accessing conversations about your company or brand. If a traveler posts an update to Twitter that there are no dining options at XYZ airport other than fast-food concessions, then an airport representative monitoring the airport's social media presence can respond to the customer with the names and locations of food and beverage outlets offering healthy alternatives to fast food.

. . .

As demonstrated throughout this chapter, sharing unique knowledge embodies three truths of exceptional customer service:

1. It reflects the essence—the most critical aspect, the highest priority—of every service industry employee's job role.
2. It is always voluntary. An employee *chooses* to acquire and share unique knowledge.
3. There is no additional cost. Unique knowledge is free to share.

Consider the job role of the luggage salesperson who sold me the Tumi garment bag. Like every salesperson's job, it is made up of two parts: job function and job essence. The salesperson I encountered at the first luggage store demonstrated her job knowledge (job function) when she answered, "The only time I've seen these bags discounted is when a color or style has been discontinued" in response to my question about whether Tumi bags ever went on sale.

But the salesperson I encountered at the second luggage store demonstrated both job knowledge (job function) as well as unique knowledge (job essence) by sharing product knowledge beyond that which might reasonably be expected by the consumer.

Salespeople are *required* to learn job knowledge about the products they sell, such as product specifications, features, and benefits. However, the second salesperson's decisions to obtain and then share an additional layer of product knowledge (unique knowledge) in order to better serve customers were *voluntary* decisions. She didn't have to take these extra steps, and most salespeople don't.

How much did it cost for the second salesperson to share the unique knowledge she had acquired about Tumi's unique product warranty and Tracer® recovery system? *There is no additional cost to share unique knowledge.* It's true that it does take time for salespeople to acquire an additional layer of product knowledge. But now they are more prepared to represent the product to prospective customers in a way that neutralizes their objections and reinforces the product's value. In this way, the salesperson's investment in acquiring unique knowledge pays for itself over and over again.

GETTING FROM ORDINARY TO EXTRAORDINARY

- Job knowledge is sufficient to meet expectations and satisfy customers, but unique knowledge is required if your goal is to exceed expectations and delight customers.
- Job knowledge informs employees so that they can execute their job functions accurately, safely, and efficiently. It is required of employees and expected by customers. It resides in training programs and policy and procedure manuals.
- Unique knowledge enables employees to reflect job essence, their highest priority at work. Unique knowledge is not required of employees and is not expected by customers.

- Unique knowledge exceeds the knowledge typically associated with a job role. Most often, unique knowledge is not found in a book or manual. It has character and substance.
- Employees voluntarily acquire unique knowledge and share it with customers and coworkers.
- Unique knowledge, when acquired by employees and shared with customers, can mean the difference between executing predictable transactions and providing refreshing service experiences.
- While customers appreciate nice employees, they value knowledgeable employees. And the more unique knowledge employees possess, the more value they bring to the customer experience.
- Unique knowledge is captivating. When exposed to it, customers tend to concentrate and listen intently.
- Unique knowledge creates sales. Because it is special and unexpected, it is more likely to make a lasting positive impression on customers and influence sales.
- Unique knowledge provides an "insider's" perspective. This "peek behind the curtain" builds immediate rapport with customers and reinforces their personal importance.
- When employees' job knowledge about a company's products or services exceeds that which might reasonably be expected of them, it becomes unique knowledge.
- Acquiring unique knowledge about the competition does not require covert operations and night-vision goggles. Practicing humility, candor, and graciousness toward competitors creates an environment of openness and trust. There is a willingness, even an enthusiasm, to share unique knowledge with the goal of improving the product and service quality offered to customers.
- Companies can acquire unique knowledge about their customers by soliciting or otherwise noting their preferences, storing the data, and then retrieving the information to better serve them at a later date.

- Sharing unique knowledge reflects the essence—the most critical aspect, the highest priority—of every service industry employee's job role.
- Sharing unique knowledge is always voluntary. An employee *chooses* to acquire and share unique knowledge.
- There is no additional cost to share unique knowledge. It's free.

Applying Unique Knowledge

In the space provided, record examples of how you can apply concepts from the chapter to raise customer service quality that you deliver or influence from ordinary to extraordinary!

ORDINARY	EXTRAORDINARY
Say, "Here you go" as a customer pulls up to the drive-through window to retrieve her espresso drink.	Say, "Here's your espresso macchiato. Did you know that macchiato means 'marked' or 'stained' in Italian? The espresso is 'marked' with a teaspoon of milk."
◦	◦
◦	◦
◦	◦
◦	◦

5

Convey Authentic Enthusiasm

Enthusiasm is a word that conjures up different associations depending on whom you are talking to, so let's just consider its literal definition: *great excitement for or interest in a subject or cause.* Like most of us, I have experienced highs and lows in life. I have discovered that being enthusiastic comes naturally to me during the high points but requires more effort during the low points. But regardless of how things are going, I know that I have the freedom to choose my response and that enthusiasm is always among my options.

Years ago, I attended a seminar based on the seminal book by the late Stephen R. Covey, *The 7 Habits of Highly Effective People*. While studying the first habit—Be Proactive—I was exposed to a model of what Covey called the four human endowments (or gifts):

1. **Self-awareness:** our knowledge of self; our personal thoughts, moods, and tendencies
2. **Imagination:** the ability to shape our own thoughts beyond our present reality

3. **Conscience:** our awareness of what is right and wrong
4. **Independent will:** our ability to act on our own self-awareness, free from external influences

Covey suggested that, as human beings, we could capitalize on one or more of these endowments in order to respond positively rather than react negatively to a given situation.

Responding enthusiastically resides in the human endowment of imagination. As human beings, when faced with a difficult situation, we have the ability to employ our imagination and choose our response to negative stimuli. So, even though our present reality might appear bleak, we can exercise our imagination and convey authentic enthusiasm in response to the negative event.

The late Norman Vincent Peale, author of *The Power of Positive Thinking*, said, "Think enthusiastically about everything; but especially your job. If you do, you'll put a touch of glory in your life. If you love your job with enthusiasm, you'll shake it to pieces. You'll love it into greatness."

The problem is that most people don't love their jobs. According to Sirota Consulting, experts in employee attitude research, of all the organizations they have surveyed, "only 13.8 percent can be categorized as having an 'enthusiastic' workforce." Sirota defines an enthusiastic workforce as one whose needs are met for equity, achievement, and camaraderie.

Volumes have been written on ways to stimulate employees, increase their job satisfaction, and create an enthusiastic and engaged workforce. These include *The Enthusiastic Employee* (by David Sirota, Louis Mischkind, and Michael Irwin Meltzer), *Love 'Em or Lose 'Em* (by Beverly Kaye and Sharon Jordan-Evans), *The Carrot Principle* (by Adrian Gostick and Chester Elton), and *How Full Is Your Bucket?* (by Tom Rath and Donald Clifton).

For the purposes of this chapter, I would like to debunk the notion that an enthusiastic employee is one who is overly animated, possessing unbridled levels of energy, and wears a permanent smile to convey his perpetual state of happiness. While these traits are compatible with customer service roles, they are unique to individuals who feel comfortable displaying them while interacting with and serving customers. In fact, you may know people who fit this description and are well suited to their job roles.

Consider the best customer service that you have received recently. If you were to create a short list of adjectives to describe the service provider responsible, you may include descriptors such as professional, knowledgeable, efficient, savvy, or courteous. Regardless of how you described the individual, an employee who conveys authentic enthusiasm does so in a way that is unique, perhaps even singular, and matches his style and personality. And while this may be animated or may be reserved, it will be real.

The first exceptional service behavior described in this book, *express genuine interest*, emphasizes genuineness, and the second behavior, *offer sincere and specific compliments*, emphasizes sincerity. Likewise, the fourth behavior, *convey authentic enthusiasm*, reinforces authenticity. Exceptional customer service is never predicated on superficiality or disingenuousness. If a service provider's smile reverts to an indifferent expression the moment a customer turns away, that demonstrates duplicity. Exceptional customer service is not about masking your true feelings. It's about actualizing them.

The Role of Leadership in Fostering Authentic Enthusiasm

If it's true that less than 14 percent of organizations surveyed have an enthusiastic workforce, then leadership has its work cut out for it. However, it would be a mistake for a manager to establish the goal of "build an enthusiastic workforce." There are just too many variables. It would be better to focus on smaller, more manageable processes that, when individually addressed, can influence the enthusiasm level of a workforce. One example is to learn your employees' passions and interests outside work in order to use that information to foster enthusiasm at work. Another is to reinforce enthusiasm in the workplace through ongoing training and by consistently modeling desired behavior.

Learn What Your Employees Are Passionate About

The best way to create the conditions that enable an employee to convey authentic enthusiasm at work is to ensure that there is a match between what she values doing in her personal time and what she's doing at work. Think about it: If it were possible to harness the same feelings and attitudes that employees have toward hobbies or interests outside work and display them in their roles as service providers, how might that impact customer interactions, the length of the workday, job satisfaction, and job performance?

One of the biggest responsibilities that leaders have is to make sure they have the right people in the right job roles. The only way to accomplish this is to get to know your employees. Your employees have passions and interests that can be identified only if you express genuine interest in them, ask thoughtful questions, and actively listen to their responses. Doing so may uncover employees' passions or interests outside work that could transfer to their job roles at work:

- A salesperson who is passionate about reading books outside work may share that she has a voracious appetite for gaining knowledge. She could apply this zeal for learning at work by reading up on her company's products and services and sharing that unique knowledge with coworkers and customers.
- A bus driver who is a die-hard sports fan can share his enthusiasm for sports with like-minded customers. In the process, common ground is established and relationships are formed.
- A restaurant server who looks forward to laboring in the kitchen for hours to prepare an exquisite meal for friends can apply the same mentality toward her "labor" on behalf of restaurant guests in order to create a memorable dining experience.
- A hardware store employee whose hobbies include carpentry, masonry, or landscaping can apply the same enthusiasm when advising customers who are considering their own home improvement projects.

Or maybe employees' personal interests have little to do with their work. Not all employees' passions fit neatly into their present job roles. Figuring out how they do fit simply requires some creativity. For example, consider Karen, a receptionist at a dental office, whose passion outside work is health and fitness. Naturally, if she worked as a personal trainer at Lifetime Fitness, her personal and professional interests would be aligned. But, as a receptionist, Karen's job requires sitting much of the day while greeting patients, entering data, and filing insurance claims. How can her manager channel Karen's passion for physical fitness to increase her enthusiasm for serving patients? There are several ways:

- It's easy to validate the connection between dental health and overall health. For instance, doctors have discovered a link between poor oral health and diabetes, heart disease, cancer, and more. As the ambassador for the dental office, the receptionist can reinforce the correlation between proper oral hygiene and her passion—health and fitness.
- Perhaps the dental office offers an opt-in monthly e-newsletter to its patients. The newsletter can provide an opportunity for Karen to share a nutritious, calcium-fortified smoothie recipe.
- Most cities promote an annual 5/10K race. Often, these races support worthy charities or causes. Assuming she plans to register for the race, show your support by sponsoring Karen and encouraging her to share her enthusiasm for the event with patients.

By identifying links between employees' passions outside work and their job responsibilities at work, it's possible for managers to create working environments where employees naturally convey authentic enthusiasm for serving customers.

Reinforce Enthusiasm in Your Workplace

Enthusiasm is contagious. So is a lack of enthusiasm. Leaders have a responsibility to reinforce performance standards and expectations by providing ongoing training that is more frequent and less formal and by consistently modeling desired behavior.

Effective leaders recognize that if they wait six months for the next formal classroom training opportunity to discuss customer service, they have waited too long. Customer service benefits from more frequent, daily training before every shift as a part of informal pre-shift meetings. For instance, a call center manager might say, "Today, I'd like us to make a special effort to pleasantly surprise customers by conveying authentic enthusiasm for serving them." She could then involve her team by posing questions such as "What does it look like to convey authentic enthusiasm?" or "What are some ways that you currently convey authentic enthusiasm to callers?"

Through participation, her team can identify numerous examples of what it looks like to convey authentic enthusiasm and of ways team members currently convey authentic enthusiasm to callers. The manager could also share her own ideas based on her unique background. The act of simply talking about conveying authentic enthusiasm increases employees' awareness and leads to more engaging interactions with customers.

But it doesn't stop there. Employees are always watching their immediate supervisors for cues on how they should act. In a call center environment, for instance, if employees observe their supervisor neglecting to smile into the phone and add enthusiasm to his voice during customer calls, then they too may view these behaviors as optional. Even worse, the supervisor now loses credibility with the staff, which devalues any future conversations pertaining to customer service.

Great service starts with great leadership. If you are in a leadership role, it is essential that you model the customer service standards and expectations that are communicated to your frontline staff. Whether you do or don't, they are always watching.

How to Convey Authentic Enthusiasm

Most customer service interactions are not laced with poor performance, rude behavior, or excessive inaccuracies. More often, these encounters are simply routine and transactional. When employees convey authentic enthusiasm, it's like a breath of fresh air to customers who have come to expect indifference. Enthusiasm is irresistible to customers, is good for business, and leaves a lasting positive impression.

Be Compelling

Customers no longer expect an enthusiastic reception from employees. They have been lulled into complacency by many years of predictable, process-focused customer service, devoid of originality and enthusiasm. When employees break with tradition by conveying authentic enthusiasm, customers take notice.

A year ago, at my son's football camp, I noticed that whenever he went out for a pass during scrimmage, he'd stop, wave his arms wildly, and call out to the quarterback, "I'm open! I'm open!"

The quarterback would glance in Cooper's direction and see what the rest of us saw—the defender standing just behind Cooper, ready to intercept the pass—and he'd either throw to a different receiver or run the ball.

Cooper was clearly becoming frustrated. During a break in the scrimmage, I approached him and shared this advice: "Coop, if you want the quarterback to throw you the ball, you must give him a reason to. You need to make yourself a *compelling* target."

At the time, Cooper was eight years old, so I defined "compelling" for him as commanding attention, having a powerful and irresistible effect.

It occurred to me that this advice applies to business as well. Whether large organizations or sole proprietorships, companies must give prospective customers a reason to consider doing business with them. They must make themselves compelling in order to attract attention, differentiate themselves from competitors, and, ultimately, close sales. One way for employees to distinguish themselves is by being intentional about conveying authentic enthusiasm.

Whenever I think about this service behavior, I think about the sign spinners near major intersections. It's the responsibility of these employees to entice motorists to turn at the intersection in order to take advantage of a lunch special, a clearance sale, or the best rate offered for selling your gold jewelry.

Have you noticed the disparity between sign spinners? Some are no more than human billboards who passively hold the sign in one hand while texting with the other. But others choose to be compelling and convey authentic enthusiasm by choreographing dance moves that complement the spinning of their signs. If you are the business owner who is employing the sign spinner to attract the attention of motorists and increase your store's traffic (and, presumably, its sales), which employee would you hire?

New York City is renowned for many things, including cheesecake. If you are a provider of cheesecake and are planning to compete in this category, then you'd better bring your "A" game because the competition is tough! Here's an example of someone who is definitely bringing her "A" game.

CASE STUDY: A BAKERY PROVIDING DELIGHT FOR CUSTOMERS

Last year, I met Eileen Avezzano, the owner of Eileen's Special Cheesecake in New York City. She has been making cheesecake the old-fashioned way, using her mother's original recipe, for nearly four decades! According to Eileen, "I don't feel any less enthusiastic today than I did when I sold my first cheesecake thirty-nine years ago!"

I asked her what, besides the product itself, distinguishes her bakery from an ordinary bakery. "One thing that's different," Eileen says, "is that I invite customer interaction. I refuse to place signs on everything and expect customers to answer their own questions. At most bakeries, it becomes a reading exercise for customers. Every item in the display case has its own little tag with the product name, ingredients, and price."

Customers at these bakeries are expected to locate and point to what they want. The employee then packs it up, charges them, and moves on to the next customer in line. This type of environment often produces a factory mentality focused on executing job function, treating each customer like the last customer. Have a question? Read the sign.

"We're not reliant on signs," insists Eileen. "We offer a personal experience over the counter. We serve people from all over the world. And these customers don't all speak English. During any given hour in our store, we may serve customers speaking seven or eight different languages. I insist that employees go through each of the flavors. Customers can ask any questions they want. Our employees will answer them and make sure they get exactly what they are looking for."

Although this approach may not be as efficient as labeling each product in the display case, Eileen contends that it is ultimately more effective. By engaging customers as opposed to referring them to signage, employees have a chance to establish rapport and make lasting positive impressions on customers that can extend the relationship beyond a onetime transaction inside the store—even if the customers are not local. Because Eileen's Special Cheesecake ships to all fifty states and Puerto Rico, delighted customers from out of town can repurchase again and again.

The comedian Steve Martin once said, "Be so good they can't ignore you." Whether going out for a pass, spinning a sign, or selling cheesecake, if your front-facing service providers are not compelling, then they are likely to be disregarded. Instead of differentiating themselves and the brand they represent, they blend into the scenery. And instead of being irresistible, they are going to be ignored.

Be Likeable

People buy from people they like. When employees express genuine interest in customers by making eye contact, smiling, and adding energy to their voices, they are conveying authentic enthusiasm for serving them. These service providers are infinitely more engaging and likeable than those who appear preoccupied or indifferent, and their sales prove it.

The following story shows how a program to increase add-on sales wound up energizing an entire staff and filling the workers with enthusiasm.

CASE STUDY: A SUCCESSFUL INCENTIVE PROGRAM

A few years ago, I met a Paradise Bakery & Cafe general manager named Sandy Jones who told me about an incentive program she had introduced to increase add-on sales of bottled water, cookies, and other high-margin items at her unit, which was located in a mall food court. She worked with vendors to sponsor the prizes, ranging from iTunes gift cards to iPods.

Employees were so energized by the incentive program that they constantly asked Sandy to print the sales report to assess how they were performing compared to their coworkers. The report was the only way that employees could see who on the team was producing the most add-on sales.

That gave Sandy an idea. Instead of letting people know how they were performing only when the report was printed, she decided to hoot and holler while clanking a stainless steel container with a metal spoon to acknowledge, in the moment, when one of her team members had contributed add-on sales.

In doing so, Sandy included an element of spontaneous recognition to the incentive program. This not only created additional enthusiasm among team members—it also created a stir with customers in the food court, who were taken with what the employees were doing to entertain them. All of sudden, customers were coming by to see what all the clanking and laughter was about. This increased the unit's traffic and capture rate in a highly competitive environment with plenty of other dining options from which to choose.

A couple of weeks into the promotion, the staff got together and bought Sandy a cowbell to use in place of her makeshift noisemaker. That day, she earned the nickname Cowbell Sandy. Over time, the incentive program proved to be a huge success. Top producers were contributing more than $11 an hour in add-on sales in a high-energy environment teeming with enthusiasm, recognition, and sales!

Here's another true story that illustrates return on enthusiasm (ROE).

CASE STUDY: ELEMENTARY SCHOOL ENTHUSIASM

Two little girls from a neighborhood elementary school stopped by a local office building to sell candy for a school fundraiser. Each of the girls was toting a rather large bag filled with boxes of candy. Several employees who had seen their school bus pull up gathered in the reception area to greet the girls. One girl was kind of shy and didn't say two words. The other one, small but confident, was as memorable as any little salesperson you ever met.

The small girl introduced herself and her partner, mentioned the school they represented, and asked if anyone would like to buy candy for their fundraiser. One of the employees said, "I don't have any money with me today, sorry." Not missing a beat, the girl said, "We take checks!" That was sale number one as the woman made her selection and went for her checkbook.

Another employee said, "I'm on a diet and can't eat candy." The girl immediately said, "We take contributions!" and received a $5 bill. As others came up with excuses, the little girl enthusiastically overcame each objection.

She then turned to the last employee, who asked what she would win if she and her partner sold the most candy. Her face lit up as she answered, "I get to help the special children board their bus to go to camp!" The last employee bought $20 worth.

And to those readers who might dismiss this as an entertaining but soft illustration that pertains only to elementary school fundraisers, be assured that conveying authentic enthusiasm applies whether you're selling candy bars, bottles of wine, aeration services, cars, homes, or jet airplanes!

Leave a Lasting Positive Impression

Chances are that you don't recall most of the interactions you've had with retail clerks, airline flight attendants, or bank tellers that you might describe as transactional. But it's a safe bet that you can remember those interactions you have had over the years that were noticeably different. Something stood out. Perhaps it was the service provider's presence or that he made you feel especially important. Perhaps he added uniqueness and flair to an ordinary process and, in doing so, made it memorable and left a lasting positive impression.

I once ordered an omelet at an omelet station at a hotel in Atlanta. The omelet maker was wearing a starched white apron that he had meticulously pressed with an accordion-like pattern. It was so remarkable that you had to ask him about it.

When I did ask him, he commented that all the aprons look alike, so he gets up a few minutes early each morning in order to press the unique pattern into his apron. He said he receives frequent comments from hotel guests on his enhanced apron, and that on many occasions, his apron sparks conversations that otherwise would not have occurred.

Although this was ten years ago, I still recall his name, Ulysses. Seriously, how many of you can recall these types of details from a single interaction you had with an omelet maker, or another service provider, a decade ago? Ulysses used his customized uniform to convey authentic enthusiasm for serving customers in a way that is unique, perhaps even singular, and matched his style and personality.

Hayward Spears is the owner of a barbeque restaurant in Overland Park, Kansas. He also displays authentic enthusiasm for his work. I remember Hayward from when I was ten years old. During the summer months when we were out of school, my friends and I used to walk to a local shopping center to buy packs of gum or candy bars, whatever we could get for two quarters.

I remember how hot the summers were in Kansas and how we would always end up at Hayward's Pit Barbeque, a cramped restaurant at the corner of 95th and Antioch. Hayward Spears was the owner, cook, cashier, table busser, and dishwasher. Our motley crew of sweaty kids would step inside the air-conditioned restaurant to cool off with no intention of buying anything.

Although the tiny restaurant had just five stools and four booths, we were always made to feel welcome. Rather than running us out to create room for paying customers, Hayward conveyed authentic enthusiasm for serving us by presenting us with a tray full of textured red and gold plastic cups filled with ice water, the condensation trickling down the sides.

Hayward conveys his enthusiasm in a February 2011 interview in *The Best Times*, a local monthly newspaper in Johnson County, Kansas. He said:

> "[While working two jobs] I was pursuing my real passion, which was barbecue. I'd gotten interested as a kid watching my dad. He would butcher a pig, barbecue the whole pig on an open pit in our back yard, and smoke it in our smoke house. Barbecuing just stayed with me, and I developed a love for it and a real passion. On weekends here in Kansas City, I would barbecue for family and friends and my church, over an open pit I dug in our own back yard. I developed my own techniques."

A few years ago when I was back in Overland Park on business, I stopped by Hayward's as I always do when I'm in town. This time, to my delight, I saw Hayward personally greeting customers inside the entryway of his present location! I introduced myself and shared my memories of him and his original restaurant from the mid-1970s. I told him that, even though Kansas City is filled with quality barbeque restaurants, I always return to his restaurant because of the treatment I received three decades earlier as a sweaty kid on summer break.

Not surprisingly, he has heard similar stories from other customers who go out of their way to buy his barbeque. In fact, Hayward's is so popular that they are now serving more than 5,000 customers a week!

Hayward's comment that he began his barbeque empire by first serving family and friends demonstrates that conveying authentic enthusiasm as well as every other exceptional customer service behavior can be applied both at work and at home to leave lasting positive impressions.

. . .

Several years ago, after the birth of our first child, I began pouring pancake batter into unique shapes that our son would recognize. When he was very young, I poured shapes ranging from puppies to pacifiers. As he grew older, I adapted the shapes to his interests, whether dinosaurs or chess pieces.

Holidays always provided fodder for themed shapes. I began pouring shamrocks in March, firecrackers in July, jack-o'-lanterns in October, and candy canes in December. As our family grew, all of our children looked forward to these pancakes and enjoyed requesting made-to-order shapes. Breakfasts transformed from a predictable meal, a base to be touched each morning, to a festive event where the family lingers and memories are made.

I got to thinking about how this equates to customer service. According to research by the consulting firm Beyond Philosophy, 44 percent of consumers described the majority of customer service experiences they have as "bland and uneventful." These are the process-focused transactions that are marked by apathy, routine, and indifference. As it applies to breakfast, it's like eating a bowl of Corn Flakes. Even though you have eaten and may even be satisfied, you are not going to remember it.

Contrast an ordinary bowl of Corn Flakes with pancakes in the shapes of dinosaurs, chess pieces, or whatever shapes are meaningful to you. Would you describe shaped pancakes as "bland and uneventful?" Is a pancake in the shape of a rook forgettable if you are a chess enthusiast? Which breakfast experience is likely to make a lasting positive impression?

Families are busy. I have four children. I understand that it's impractical to make shaped pancakes every day. (Besides, if you did, they might lose some of their magic.) Most mornings we have cereal or frozen waffles because these meals are easier and more efficient. Even so, I am intentional about planning for the mornings that I make shaped pancakes. It's my unique way of expressing genuine interest in my children and conveying authentic enthusiasm for serving them.

How does this concept apply to your business? How does it apply to your life? Be deliberate about conveying authentic enthusiasm for serving others and, in the process, transform products, services, events, and relationships from process-focused, routine, and predictable to something much, much more.

Just like shaped pancakes, the possibilities are endless.

As revealed throughout this chapter, conveying authentic enthusiasm embodies three truths of exceptional customer service:

1. It reflects the essence—the most critical aspect, the highest priority—of every service industry employee's job role.
2. It is always voluntary. An employee *chooses* to convey authentic enthusiasm.
3. There is no additional cost. Enthusiasm is free.

Consider, again, the example of Eileen Avezzano. Like every bakeshop employee, her job role is made up of two parts: job function and job essence. Eileen and the other bakeshop employees are expected to execute job functions such as baking products, filling display cases, and ringing up purchases. But they are also expected to demonstrate job essence by not relying on those little tags in the display case (which become surrogates for employee interaction). Without those little tags, they can create opportunities to engage customers, elicit questions, and ultimately sell more cheesecake by conveying authentic enthusiasm for the product itself and for serving customers.

Eileen performs both job function and job essence by not only filling display cases (job function) but by doing so while smiling, making eye contact, and, with enthusiasm in her voice, asking, "What questions do you have?" (job essence). Not only does she demonstrate job knowledge (the *what*) and skill (the *how*) that bakery customers expect, she also reflects purpose (the *why*) that customers do not always expect. According to Eileen, her purpose—to make people happy—is reinforced every time she hears a customer say, "It wouldn't be a holiday or special occasion without an Eileen's Special Cheesecake!"

Bakeshop employees are *required* to execute mandatory job functions. It's what they were hired to do. It's what they are paid to do. However, Eileen's choice to convey authentic enthusiasm for serving her customers by creating opportunities for engagement is a *voluntary* decision. She doesn't have to invite questions. Most bakeshop employees don't.

How much does it cost for Eileen to convey authentic enthusiasm for serving customers? There is no additional cost. Enthusiasm is free!

Enthusiasm is a gift. One of Stephen Covey's four human endowments, imagination, enables us to convey authentic enthusiasm in response to any negative event. Some people display enthusiasm in a way that is demonstrative. Others are more reserved. Regardless, authenticity is key.

Leaders are responsible for getting to know their employees, identifying their passions and interests outside work, and creating a work environment where employees naturally convey authentic enthusiasm for serving customers. Leaders must also reinforce enthusiasm in the workplace by providing ongoing training that is more frequent and less formal and by modeling the expected behaviors daily.

When employees convey authentic enthusiasm for serving customers, customers feel appreciated and believe that their business is valued.

GETTING FROM ORDINARY TO EXTRAORDINARY

- Human beings have the freedom to choose their response to any situation, and enthusiasm is always among their options.
- Author Stephen R. Covey suggested that, as human beings, we can capitalize on one or more human endowments—self-awareness, independent will, conscience, and imagination—in order to respond positively rather than react negatively to a given situation. Responding enthusiastically resides in the human endowment of imagination.
- An employee who conveys authentic enthusiasm does so in a way that is unique, perhaps even singular, and matches his style and personality. And while this may be animated or may be reserved, it is real.
- Exceptional customer service is not about masking your true feelings. It's about actualizing them.
- The best way to create the conditions for an employee to convey authentic enthusiasm at work is to ensure that there is a match between what she values doing in her personal time and what she's doing at work.

- Conveying authentic enthusiasm is irresistible to customers, good for business, and leaves a lasting positive impression.
- Great service starts with great leadership. If you are in a leadership role, it is essential that you model the customer service standards and expectations that are communicated to your frontline staff.
- According to research by the consulting firm Beyond Philosophy, 44 percent of consumers described the majority of customer service experiences they have as "bland and uneventful."
- Conveying authentic enthusiasm reflects the essence—the most critical aspect, the highest priority—of every service industry employee's job role.
- Conveying authentic enthusiasm is always voluntary. An employee *chooses* to convey authentic enthusiasm.
- There is no additional cost. Conveying authentic enthusiasm to others is free.

Applying Authentic Enthusiasm

In the space provided, record examples of how you can apply concepts from the chapter to raise customer service quality that you deliver or influence from ordinary to extraordinary!

ORDINARY	EXTRAORDINARY
Place signage in the bakery display case with the intent to limit interaction between customers and service providers.	Remove signage from the bakery display case to encourage interaction between customers and service providers.
•	•
•	•
•	•
•	•

6

Use Appropriate Humor

Business is supposed to be serious, right? To succeed in business requires serious attributes such as persistence, commitment, and dedication. If employees want to be taken seriously by company executives and customers, they would be advised to avoid spontaneity and humor in favor of strict compliance with established corporate norms. Sounds a bit Orwellian, doesn't it?

Although the above description of business may seem harsh, in the case of most companies, there is at least some truth to it. Unless a company and its employees are intentional about using appropriate humor— humor that is suitable or fitting for a particular purpose, person, or occasion—in service situations, like every other exceptional customer service behavior highlighted in this book, it is left to chance. And when aspects of business are left to chance, the frequency with which they occur is less than when they are a recognized part of the service culture by design.

Southwest Airlines and Trader Joe's are examples of companies that are intentional about infusing appropriate humor into their customer interactions. Southwest Airlines flight attendants have earned a reputation for adding levity to their in-flight announcements (which you will have an opportunity to sample later in this chapter). And Trader Joe's employees don Hawaiian shirts, use a bell in place of a public address system, and think grocery shopping should be a pleasurable experience rather than another chore to endure.

At my public seminars, I often solicit examples of what participants and their companies are currently doing to encourage an element of levity and a demonstration of light-heartedness in their service culture. I am routinely dismayed at the number of participants who cannot identify a single example. It really is a missed opportunity for these employees to realize the benefits of using humor to make their customers' experiences with them more enjoyable and memorable. As Charlie Chaplin said, "A day without laughter is a day wasted."

Displaying a sense of humor doesn't mean that employees need to force joyfulness or call undue attention to themselves in the workplace. They just need to be open to opportunities to introduce comic relief that everyday life provides, like the following example from my local Starbucks drive-through. One morning, I pulled up to the speaker to place my coffee order. The conversation went something like this:

ME: "I'd like a Double Shot with Energy." (Energy is a supplement that Starbucks adds to its beverages upon request.)

BARISTA *(in a monotone voice)*: "I'm sorry but we're out of Energy this morning."

ME: "Yeah, I can hear it in your voice."

BARISTA *(with enthusiasm in his voice)*: "Oh, wait! I lied. I found some more Energy!"

ME: "Yeah, I can hear it in your voice."

I then pulled up to the drive-through window where I was greeted by the barista.

BARISTA: "Was that a *Grande* Double Shot with Energy?"

ME: "Yes. Sorry—I don't think I mentioned the size."

BARISTA: "That's okay. I'm psychic. I heard it in your voice."

Ba-DUM bump!

Compare this exchange with a typical dry, lifeless interaction that you would expect to have at a quick-service restaurant. What's different about it? It requires initiative. When presented with an opportunity to add levity, the barista seized the moment. By contrast, at most drive-throughs, the transaction is executed without a hint of personality, and one day's visit is indistinguishable from the next.

Using appropriate humor is an effective way for employees to incorporate their unique personality into their job roles. Instead of settling for the monotony of executing job functions and treating each customer like the last customer, employees can reflect their own unique style and flair by taking the initiative to add levity to their service interactions.

When to Use Appropriate Humor

Assuming they do not work as grief counselors, funeral parlor directors, or soldiers in the Queen's Guard (in which case their opportunities to use humor are somewhat diminished, if not eliminated altogether), there are a variety of circumstances when it can be advantageous and appropriate for employees to add levity to their jobs. Whether to establish rapport with customers, to enliven ordinary processes that customers have come to expect, to make lasting positive impressions on their customers, or to reduce tension during a conflict, using humor is an effective way for employees to raise customer experiences from ordinary to extraordinary.

Use Humor to Establish Rapport

When employees encounter customers for the first time, it is incumbent upon them to make them feel comfortable. One way to establish rapport with customers, as discussed in Chapter 2, is by expressing genuine interest in them. Another way to casually build rapport is by using appropriate humor.

Comedian Victor Borge said, "Laughter is the shortest distance between two people." Successful bartenders are well aware of this, and many of them have earned reputations for sharing one-liners to break

the ice with patrons and set the tone for an evening of good cheer. Let's see if any of these classics have a similar effect on you:

- A skeleton walks into a bar and says, "Bartender, I'll have a beer and a mop."
- A termite walks into a bar and asks, "Is the bar tender here?"
- A three-legged dog walks into a bar in the Old West and says, "I'm here to find the man who shot my paw."
- A horse walks into a bar and the bartender asks, "So, why the long face?"

When combined with knowledge, humor enhances expertise, demonstrating confidence and competency. But using appropriate humor to build rapport with customers is not limited to bartenders. Here are a few more examples I have encountered recently:

- Our waiter at the View Restaurant & Lounge in New York City added a spark to the otherwise routine water order when he asked, "Which would you prefer with your meal? (*said in an upbeat voice*) A bottle of San Pellegrino sparkling mineral water, or (*said in a monotone*) New York City tap?" (I almost never select the bottled water, but on this occasion, I ordered two.)
- After my father-in-law requested chopsticks at the Shanghai Garden Chinese Restaurant in Centennial, Colorado, the hostess asked, "Are you left- or right-handed?"
- One of the fishmongers at the world-famous Pike Place Fish Market in Seattle, responding to a customer's inquiry about whether

or not credit cards were accepted as she placed her selection on the counter, said, "Sure. Would you like *two*?" (The customer paused for a moment to consider the question, then broke out in laughter.)

- Our server at the Summit Steakhouse in Aurora, Colorado, after introducing the specials, said, "If you have any questions, don't hesitate to ask." Then, as he patted his rotund belly, he added, "As you can see, I have a *lot* of product knowledge!"

In each case, by substituting levity for a predictable response, these service providers established a connection with their customers. Rather than simply executing another transaction that would soon be forgotten, they each used their unique personalities to create a lasting positive impression.

Use Humor to Enliven Ordinary Processes

Appropriate humor can also be used when you want to enliven the ordinary, mundane procedures inherent in your particular business.

One way of doing this is to engage customers with something other than providing the same customary and expected information. A great opportunity for this is airlines' in-flight announcements and safety briefings. In the past, passengers compliantly listened to uneventful briefings where the only deviation from the expected might be the pilot's announcement about some interesting geographical feature viewable from one side of the aircraft. Then, along came Southwest Airlines, whose flight attendants began interjecting humor into their briefings to soothe restive passengers and increase the likelihood that they would actually listen to the monotonous safety announcements that they might otherwise tune out. More recently, United Airlines and others have allowed flight attendants to deviate from rigid scripts and pepper their announcements with personality. Below are examples from a variety of airlines:

- "To operate your seat belt, insert the metal tab into the buckle and pull tight. It works just like every other seat belt, and if you don't know how to operate one, you probably shouldn't be out in public unsupervised."

- "In the event of a sudden loss of cabin pressure, oxygen masks will drop from the compartment above. To start the flow of oxygen, simply insert your credit card . . ."
- "Once the oxygen masks have deployed, stop screaming, grab the mask, and pull it over your face. If you have a small child traveling with you, secure your mask before assisting with theirs. If you are traveling with more than one small child, then pick your favorite."
- "Weather at our destination is 70 degrees with some broken clouds, but we'll try to have them fixed by the time we arrive."
- "Your seat cushion may be used as a flotation device. In the unlikely event of an emergency water landing, please paddle to shore and take it home with our compliments."
- "At this time, please turn off all portable electronic devices. This includes anything that starts with an 'i' or ends with a 'Berry.' "
- "As you exit the plane, please make sure to gather all of your belongings. Anything left behind will be distributed evenly among the flight attendants. Please do not leave children or spouses."

Opportunities to incorporate appropriate humor are limited only by one's imagination. Humor can be added to packaging, signage, instructions, and routine processes as illustrated by the following examples.

During a recent trip to Whole Foods Market, I stopped by the seafood counter for salmon. The employee behind the counter oiled and seasoned the fillets, wrapped them in butcher paper, and handed them to me over the counter with a broad smile.

As I looked at the package, I noticed that the fish had been wrapped in customized butcher paper made to look like newsprint. Beneath the *Seafood Times* masthead were a variety of informative and entertaining stories such as "Whole Foods Market Pleads Guilty to Seafood Discrimination" and "Make Your Kitchen a Safe Harbor." The stories were laced with humor to capture the attention of shoppers.

Instead of bland and predictable brown butcher paper that I could get anywhere, I received a unique and refreshing version that could be found only at Whole Foods Market. All of a sudden, an experience that would have ended at most stores was extended to my home, as my wife and I swapped details from the different stories we read while preparing dinner.

Chipotle Mexican Grill also capitalizes on an often overlooked resource to make a positive lasting impression on its customers. Employees place to-go orders in brown bags with handles. Handles are unique (you don't see them at most quick-service restaurants), but what is truly memorable is the message printed on the bottom of its bags:

Don't throw this bag away!
   Try these other uses:
   - Cat carrier
   - Put handles over ears . . . hands-free burrito eating
   - 401(k) statements filing receptacle
   - NOT recommended as a parachute

Besides reinforcing the importance of recycling, Chipotle uses appropriate humor to enliven the ordinary process of taking food home, as well as to extend the service experience from the restaurant to the customer's home or office.

Moving on to distinctly different kinds of businesses, I recall a brokerage firm's automated voice mail message that began with typical prompts such as "For quotes, please press 1" and "To log on to the automated system, press 2." But the seventh option was unexpected: "If you'd like to hear a duck quack, press 7." Now, I've listened to my share of predictable voice mail directories, but I have never come across anything as refreshing as this. Apparently, I'm not alone. During the duck quack's heyday, the firm saw a 75 percent increase in new customers!

How about the actual instructions printed on the containers of two different body lotions? Which is more memorable?

"Directions: Use daily and reapply to rough, chapped, or ashy areas as needed. For external use only."

"Instructions for use: After showering, apply generously onto any skin that evokes warm, scaly memories of the pet iguana your cousin Danny had in seventh grade."

And think back to the last time you received an automated wake-up call at a hotel. Do you remember the message? What did it say? Perhaps it sounded something like this: "Good morning. Today's weather forecast calls for partly sunny skies, breezy, with a high temperature of 62 degrees. Thank you for choosing the XYZ hotel."

Now, compare that message with one of the tailored recordings from Hilton's theWit Hotel in Chicago, which bucks convention by offering guests a wake-up call featuring the voice of the city's most notorious mobster: "Hey you dirty rat. This is Al Capone reminding you to get your rotten bones outta that sack. Now get it moving. I've got an overdue Valentine's Day gift for Eliot Ness I gotta deliver. Heheheheh!"

Now, perhaps this form of humor doesn't fit the style or personality of your company, but that's okay. You have to do what works for your brand and clientele. The point is to be intentional about identifying ordinary processes in your business that could be energized by adding appropriate humor.

Whoever said, "It's so boring; it's like watching wallpaper dry" didn't stay at the Algonquin Hotel in New York City. Prior to its latest renovation, its guest floor wallpaper consisted of comic strips from the *New Yorker*. Hotel guests would pass the time waiting for the elevator by reading the comics. This made it difficult to keep a straight face in the elevator during the descent to the lobby (no small feat in New York City).

Also at the Algonquin, appropriate humor made its way into features as mundane as guest room door plaques. Whereas most hotels simply display a room number, the door plaque during my last stay read: "During the run of a Broadway show in which Tallulah Bankhead was starring, Heywood Broun whispered to the actress, 'Don't look now, Tallulah, but your show's slipping.'"

Throughout this book, I've emphasized that being exceptional—even unconventional—and making positive lasting impressions on customers doesn't have to cost any more than being ordinary, adhering to tradition, and providing only what is expected by customers. These examples illustrate that point. Sure, there is a cost to print on packaging, but companies are printing logos, website addresses, and instructions on packaging anyway. How much more does it cost to print something interesting and unexpected on butcher paper, a to-go bag, or a body lotion container than it costs to print something routine and predictable? Not a dime.

Look around your own business. What are some ways that you can transform products and services that are ordinary into something extraordinary using appropriate humor, design, or some other attribute?

Use Humor to Leave Lasting Positive Impressions

In the book *Made to Stick* by Chip Heath and Dan Heath, the authors propose Six Principles of Sticky Ideas that contribute to a message being retained as opposed to overlooked, disregarded, or forgotten. One of the principles is *emotions*—specifically, to make people *feel* something.

Human beings possess a complex set of emotions that are both positive and negative. Obviously, when given the chance, service providers would prefer to evoke positive emotions from their customers including amusement, delight, elation, excitement, happiness, joy, and pleasure. One of the ways to accomplish this is through humor.

Think about your current favorite sitcom. If you have friends at work who share your interest in the show, when you compare notes on the latest episode in the break room, what do people tend to recall? Likely, they remember the punch lines, funny stories, and outrageous antics delivered by the cast. They remember what made them laugh. When humor registers in the brain, it triggers endorphins that encode for memory. In a competitive environment, it is always better to be remembered than forgotten.

In recent years, I have done work for state tourism offices. When it is time for mom and dad (usually mom) to begin planning the next road trip, there are forty-nine states in the Continental United States vying for those tourism dollars. How do you suppose these states would like to be remembered by prospective customers (i.e., visitors to their states)? Consider the lasting positive impression that a parking citation issued by the city of Cheyenne, Wyoming, had on my wife.

It's happened to most of us. Your appointment ran longer than expected. You check your watch. You know it's going to be close. There is a sense of urgency as you plan your route to your parked car, weaving in and out of pedestrians on the sidewalk as you look ahead to the next crossing signal. It's flashing. If you hustle, you just might make it. A minute later, as you approach your car, you notice the piece of paper pressed beneath the windshield wiper and you think, "I'm too late." You tug the notice out from beneath the wiper blade and prepare for the worst.

This happened to my wife while she was on business in Cheyenne. She removed the notice and read the following:

Howdy Pardner!
   WELCOME TO CHEYENNE
   The Patrol Officer has noticed that you have violated one of our parking ordinances. This ordinance OVERSTAYING THE AL-LOTTED TIME is usually punishable by hanging, but seeing as how you are a visitor to Cheyenne we want to make your stay here as enjoyable as possible, so the offense will be overlooked this time. (Besides, we couldn't round up a posse in time for the hanging.)
   If we can be of any assistance during your stay in Cheyenne, please call 637-6331. If you have any comments, please fill in the area below and mail by pony express or stop by the main ranch house at 2101 O'Neil Avenue and take a look around.

What a relief! How delightfully unexpected! This may be the first time that a patrol officer brought a smile to my wife's face by leaving a notice on her windshield.

I recognize (as does the city of Cheyenne) that humor doesn't offset the expense of running a city. But it does provide a laugh and makes a lasting positive impression on visitors to Cheyenne who are likely to share this positive experience with others.

Whether you received a parking violation and fine or this "Howdy Pardner!" notice, you will likely remember the event for evoking feelings of frustration, anger, and loss in the case of a ticket, or amusement, delight, and relief in the case of this unexpected parody.

Give some thought to what you can do in your place of business to transform processes that may be creating predictably unpleasant memories (or leaving no impression at all) into something that, through the use of humor, inspires smiles and lasting positive impressions.

Use Humor to Reduce Tension

Another application of appropriate humor is to reduce tension. Health-care is an industry that presents opportunities for employees to use humor to alleviate the inevitable tension experienced by patients who are concerned about their immediate health, a forthcoming surgical procedure, or their long-term prognosis.

Aside from reducing patients' tension, there are very real health benefits stemming from the use of humor. Laughter has been called "inner jogging" because it stimulates the cardiovascular system, increases the oxygen throughout the bloodstream, and exercises the facial muscles, shoulders, diaphragm, and abdomen. While laughter itself is energizing, the residual effects create a temporary reduction in blood pressure, respiration, heart rate, and muscle tension. According to a 2004 study at the University of Maryland Medical Center, laughter, along with an active sense of humor, may reduce one's risk of a heart attack. The study found that people with heart disease were 40 percent less likely to laugh in a variety of situations compared to people of the same age without heart disease.

During the hospital stays associated with the delivery of our four children at St. Joseph Hospital in Denver, we were blessed by being served by a labor and delivery staff that recognized the calming and healing effects of using humor. We still have fond memories of the nurse who, while changing my wife's intravenous fluids, sang, "I only have IVs for you!" and the doctor who peppered his hospital room visits with corny jokes like, "Does an apple a day *really* keep the doctor away? Sure. If you aim it well enough."

Humor can also be used to reduce tension in other situations, creating smiles rather than frustration. For example, every now and then, when a server computer is inundated with requests or there is some other technical glitch, a retail transaction is delayed. If the delay is long enough, an awkward pause sets in as the customer and retail clerk await the approval and issuance of a charge slip and receipt. Ordinarily when this occurs, there is a predictable response from the service provider. Exasperated, she may roll her eyes and say, with a heavy sigh, "Sorry. The machine's been really slow today." When this occurs, the customer usually musters a faint smile in response.

What if, instead, the clerk smiled, turned an imaginary crank on the side of the register, and said to the waiting customer, "This should speed things up!" Humor in this situation may defuse tension caused by the delay and raise the customer's experience from ordinary to extraordinary.

Airports are another place where humor can be used to reduce tension, turning resistance into cooperation. While in the boarding area awaiting a United Airlines flight at Denver International Airport, I heard the voice of a gate agent over the intercom announcing that we had a very full flight and it would be necessary for a number of passengers to voluntarily check their luggage with him free of charge in order to accommodate all carry-on bags during boarding.

After two polite requests without any passengers volunteering to check their luggage, the agent—doing his best Clint Eastwood impersonation—said, "Now, see here amigos. We can do this one of two ways. Either you can turn your bags over to me, real nice like, and get a claim check, or you'll force me to fetch my lasso and take matters into my own hands. What's it gonna be, compadres?"

Amid laughter in the gate area, several smiling passengers approached the agent with their suitcases to check them before boarding.

When employees attempt to use humor to reduce the tension with incensed or frustrated customers, they must proceed with caution. It is true that adding levity can provide a much-needed distraction, bring the focus away from the anger and stress caused by negative events, and give customers a more lighthearted perspective on problems. But because of the delicate nature of certain problems, employees must use their good judgment to ensure that the humor is appropriate. Employees must make sure they do not unwittingly offend customers by appearing to be overly familiar or minimizing their problems.

In most cases, the appropriateness of whether or not to use humor under these circumstances depends on the rapport that employees have with their customers. Generally speaking, the more rapport an employee has with a customer, the greater the latitude she has to use appropriate humor in a way that will not be misinterpreted.

When the Use of Humor May Be Inappropriate

Throughout this chapter, I have shared examples of how appropriate humor has been used to raise customer service quality from ordinary to extraordinary and create lasting positive impressions in the minds of customers. Of course, *inappropriate* humor may be perceived by customers as offensive and leave lasting negative impressions. Most people do not intentionally try to offend others with their humor. Ordinarily, when humor is found to be inappropriate, it is the unintended consequence of a lapse in personal judgment or of simply being misunderstood.

Recently, I was approached by an employee of a community bank that has a branch inside my neighborhood supermarket. He decided that it would be a good idea to use the thirty-roll package of Charmin toilet tissue in my cart as a conversation starter, chuckling as he said, "I can see you got the essentials!"

I said, "Huh?" not understanding what he was referring to, to which he replied, "In my fraternity house, we never have any toilet tissue but we *always* have liquor." And he chuckled again.

Apparently, he now felt that he had built sufficient rapport to launch into his bank's mortgage refinancing options. He hadn't. In fact, he grossly misjudged his audience. I am not a twenty-something fraternity brother. I am not a peer. I am a generation removed from this overly familiar, boorish, and unprofessional "banker." Under no circumstances would I ever consider opening an account with this person, let alone entrusting him with something as significant as the mortgage on my home.

Establishing rapport with prospective customers is often the first step in attracting their business. But the way you build rapport with peers outside work is very different from the way you do so with prospective customers in a work setting—especially when other factors are present such as differences in age, gender, and ethnicity.

While lapses in personal judgment and misunderstandings are inevitable, the goal is to always use *appropriate* humor. It is understood that when interacting with customers, certain topics are off-limits, including politics, sex, religion, and—quite possibly—toilet tissue. Use your good judgment in all situations.

. . .

As illustrated throughout this chapter, using appropriate humor embodies three truths of exceptional customer service:

1. It reflects the essence—the most critical aspect, the highest priority—of every service industry employee's job role.
2. It is always voluntary. An employee *chooses* to use appropriate humor.
3. There is no additional cost. Humor is free.

Consider the job role of the barista at the Starbucks drive-through whom we met at the beginning of this chapter. Like every barista's job role, it is made up of two parts: job function and job essence. When he accepted my coffee order, he was executing job function by performing a duty associated with his job role. But when he playfully responded, "That's okay. I'm psychic. I heard it in your voice," he was displaying job essence by using appropriate humor.

Starbucks baristas are *required* to accept customers' coffee orders. (I mean, wouldn't it be awkward if they didn't?) However, his decision to play along with my sarcasm and interject humor was *voluntary*. He didn't have to use appropriate humor during our interaction. Most drive-through employees don't.

How much did it cost for the barista to use appropriate humor? *There was no additional cost*. Using appropriate humor is free!

Mark Twain said, "Humor is mankind's greatest blessing." Even so, most companies squander opportunities to incorporate appropriate humor into their products and services, choosing instead to continue the same ordinary and staid processes that customers have come to expect and take for granted. And most employees unwittingly forfeit opportunities to use appropriate humor as they dutifully execute job functions, treating each customer like the last customer.

In order to best serve customers, companies and employees must be deliberate about using appropriate humor to establish rapport with customers, enliven ordinary processes, leave lasting positive impressions, and reduce tension. At the same time, employees must be cautious not to unwittingly offend customers by using humor that is perceived to be flippant, distasteful, or overly familiar.

GETTING FROM ORDINARY TO EXTRAORDINARY

- Unless a company and its employees are intentional about using appropriate humor, it will be left to chance.
- Using appropriate humor requires initiative.
- Using appropriate humor is one way for employees to casually establish rapport with customers and make them feel comfortable.
- Adding appropriate humor can enliven ordinary processes that customers have come to expect.
- Appropriate humor can leave lasting positive impressions on customers by evoking positive emotions, including amusement, delight, elation, excitement, happiness, joy, and pleasure.
- Using appropriate humor can reduce tension caused by anxiety or, perhaps, an altercation.
- Because of the delicate nature of certain problems, employees must use their good judgment to ensure the humor is appropriate and does not unwittingly offend customers by appearing overly familiar or minimizing their problems.
- It is understood that, especially in work-related settings, certain topics are off-limits, including politics, sex, and religion.
- The use of appropriate humor reflects the essence—the most critical aspect, the highest priority—of every service industry employee's job role.
- Using appropriate humor is always voluntary. An employee *chooses* to use appropriate humor.
- There is no additional cost to use appropriate humor. Humor is free.

Applying Appropriate Humor

In the space provided, record examples of how you can apply concepts from the chapter to raise customer service quality that you deliver or influence from ordinary to extraordinary!

ORDINARY	EXTRAORDINARY
Add an automated voice mail message that provides typical prompts such as: "For hours of operation, press 1."	Add an automated voice mail message that provides an unexpected prompt such as: "If you'd like to hear a duck quack, press 7."

7

Provide Pleasant Surprises

Providing pleasant surprises presents a treasure trove of possibilities for companies and their employees to grab the attention of customers, pique their interest and curiosity, and stand out in a crowded marketplace. Surprise is an emotion whose function is to increase alertness and narrow focus. By challenging customers' assumptions and violating their expectations, powerful, indelible memories are created.

The week before Christmas two years ago, I had a morning flight out of New York's LaGuardia Airport. As I relaxed in the food court with a cup of coffee and a newspaper, I detected what appeared to be an elf approaching me. As I lowered my paper, I smiled to see a costumed entertainer who introduced herself as Kuddles the Elf.

I learned that Kuddles had been retained by the airport's management to entertain young travelers by providing complimentary balloon creations such as flowers, dinosaurs, and candy canes. Although I was not traveling with young kids, I could appreciate the welcome distraction Kuddles presented to restless children, as well as the pleasant surprise she provided to frazzled parents, who could now take a moment to catch their breath in the midst of the holiday travel gauntlet.

Providing a service that is unexpected—like an elf in an airport—may leave a greater lasting positive impression than providing service the customer already expects. Recently, my wife and I joined another couple for dinner at Mizuna in Denver. While taking our drink orders, the waiter noticed my wife's struggle to recall her preferred martini order. So he patiently walked her through her options: Gin or vodka? Dirty or not? Up or on the rocks? Olives or a lemon twist? Shaken or stirred?

Once her ideal martini was sorted out, he took the remaining drink orders and left to retrieve the cocktails. When he returned to the table a few minutes later, he provided my wife with a simple handwritten "cheat sheet" that captured all of her preferences to simplify future martini orders. What impressed me the most about his gesture was that it was completely unexpected. While I expected him to return to the table within a reasonable amount of time with accurate drink orders, I did not expect him to have a record of my wife's preferred martini order.

But surprises work both ways. The goal is to reduce the frequency with which customers experience unpleasant surprises and increase the frequency of the pleasant ones. By definition, surprises are unexpected. There are always going to be a certain number of unpleasant surprises that go undetected until customers experience them, such as the moment a restaurant guest realizes that an establishment does not accept American Express or the instant an airline passenger discovers that his seat does not recline. Unlike manufacturing, where widgets are produced in a controlled factory setting and inspected for quality *before* being made available to consumers, the service industry does not have the luxury of modifying a broken service experience ahead of time.

This fact does not, of course, preclude an organization's responsibility to obtain feedback from its customers and to continually revisit its processes to ensure that it is offering the best possible service. In addition to being intentional about reducing the number of unpleasant surprises that infiltrate existing processes, companies and their employees can also be deliberate about providing pleasant surprises.

How to Provide Pleasant Surprises

There are several ways to provide pleasant surprises that make lasting positive impressions on your customers. This might include presenting:

- Lagniappes—something given as a bonus or gift—or other "little extras" as part of your service offering (e.g., "With every pound of coffee purchased, we offer a complimentary cup of coffee or espresso drink. Which would you prefer?")
- Surprises in the moment (e.g., "Ms. Davis, I have upgraded your seat to our business class cabin. Thank you for your loyalty and enjoy your flight.")
- Surprises that are planned in advance (e.g., "We've been expecting you and have reserved a special table overlooking the harbor. Thank you for choosing to celebrate your anniversary with us.")
- Surprises as follow-up (e.g., "The day we moved into our new home, we received a stunning floral arrangement from our realtor!")

Provide Pleasant Surprises with Lagniappes or Other Little Extras

The term "lagniappe" is derived from the American Spanish phrase *la ñapa* (something that is added). The word entered the English language from Louisiana French and is chiefly used in the Gulf Coast region of the United States, where street vendors are expected to throw in "a little extra" with a purchase. For example, by adding a thirteenth pastry to an order of a dozen beignets, the merchant provides his customer with a lagniappe. Doing so has the potential to pleasantly surprise customers while adding value for the price paid. Note that the surprise can be either a tangible object (like a free sample) or an enhancement of the service.

I recently met one of the owners of Happy Cakes Bakeshop in Denver and learned that providing pleasant surprises is a part of how she conducts business. On weekdays, customers can take advantage of unadvertised discounts during Cupcake Happy Hours between 10 AM and noon.

Customers are also invited to participate in Monday Trivia Treats. Here's how it works: Every Monday, a different trivia question is posted near the register. During my most recent visit to the store, the trivia question on display was, "What was the first commercial cookie in the U.S.?"

If customers answer the question correctly, they are rewarded with a buy one, get one free bonus. When six cupcakes become a dozen, now *that's* a pleasant surprise! (Incidentally, if you guessed "Oreo" like I did, then you would have left with your original order. However, if you had guessed "Animal Crackers," then you would have been rewarded with bonus cupcakes!)

But you don't have to be a street vendor or operate a bakery in order to offer lagniappes to your customers. I recently presented to a group of self-service car wash operators. Several of them were skeptical about the relevance of pleasant surprises under the assumption that, because they did not operate full-service car washes, customer service quality was not scrutinized. They contended that as long as the equipment functioned properly, then customers would be satisfied.

I shared with the group that, while preparing for the speaking engagement, I had discovered online customer reviews about one particular self-service car wash that provides pleasant surprises for its customers by offering strawberry-scented pink foam soap and dispensing six tokens for $5 instead of five. By surprising customers with these value-added "little extras," this self-service car wash became the location of choice for many customers, who in turn attracted additional customers through their positive online reviews.

Regardless of your business, if you currently serve customers, then you can serve those customers better tomorrow by providing pleasant surprises. But you must be intentional about it. I challenge you to answer the following question and then pose it to members of your staff: *What lagniappes or "little extras" can we extend to customers that will add value to the product or service we offer while providing pleasant surprises to customers?*

Here are some recent examples of lagniappes I have encountered as a customer that added value to my service experience:

- The General Motors dealership that services my car washes it before pulling it around front and delivering it to me.

- Papa Murphy's Take 'N' Bake Pizza gives me a two-stamp head start on my pizza loyalty card. Now I'm 17 percent closer to a free pizza!
- Starbucks on occasion offers complimentary samples of ground coffee, pastries, and specialty coffee drinks.
- Tony's Market in Denver anticipates my needs by including instructions on its meat packaging (e.g., meat preparation, time frames, temperatures).
- The Wine Experience Café in Aurora, Colorado, serves its coffee tableside in French presses.
- The professional waiters at Sparks Steak House in New York City are adept at changing the table linens between entrée and dessert courses *without removing your wine glasses or exposing the tabletop*.

As previously stated, sometimes these lagniappes are tangible (e.g., Starbucks' free samples), and other times they are intangible aspects of the service experience (e.g., the changing of table linens at Sparks Steak House). In most cases, they are unexpected and transform an ordinary experience into one that is extraordinary!

Once you have identified the "little extras" that can add value to the product or service you offer, communicate them to frontline employees. To ensure consistency, update service models and processes to reflect the inclusion of these value-added pleasant surprises. By doing so, you raise the quality of customer service you currently deliver and provide enhanced value to your customers. The difference between ordinary and extraordinary really is that "little extra."

Provide Pleasant Surprises in the Moment

Pleasant surprises can also be a welcome addition to interactions employees have with customers. Too often, employees describe their work as monotonous, and customers describe their encounters with employees as transactional. Providing a pleasant surprise in the moment can disrupt the monotony of a routine transaction, making employees' jobs more satisfying and customers' experiences more memorable. Here are several examples:

- During a recent shopping trip to Target, the cashier rang up my purchases and then handed me a receipt together with a coupon for a complimentary beverage from its in-store Starbucks location.
- As I prepared to pay an $851 repair bill at the car dealership, the cashier extended a coupon for 15 percent off, saying, "This coupon will save you $123. We've partnered with the Marine Toys for Tots Foundation. If you're able to drop off an unwrapped toy in the coming week, I'll apply the coupon today."
- While using a self-service kiosk to pay for my groceries at Albertsons, I was approached by a store employee who asked if I would like a complimentary bottle of salad dressing that was being offered as a promotion. I gladly accepted and was pleasantly surprised by a free 16-ounce bottle of Kraft Light Ranch salad dressing.
- I recently returned a kitchen faucet to Lowe's that I purchased 19 months ago. Although the store's return policy is 90 days and the manufacture's warranty is 12 months, the store manager accepted the return and gave me a merchandise credit worth $171!
- At the New York Marriott Downtown, front desk agents spontaneously send guests "Connection Cards" intended to welcome them, acknowledge something they shared with the agent during check-in (e.g., reason for their hotel stay, the Broadway show they plan to see, the restaurant they plan to visit), and provide the agent's name and phone number for further assistance.

But not all pleasant surprises are formalized. Sometimes, a pleasant surprise in the moment is as simple as having your phone call answered on the first ring, having your group accommodated at a popular restaurant without a reservation, or having your luggage arrive at the baggage carousel before you do. Other times, it requires a bit more ingenuity on behalf of the service provider.

Between courses at Vesta Dipping Grill in Denver, our server provided us with a complimentary chef's taste—also known as an *amuse-bouche* (a bite-size hors d'oeuvre intended to amuse the mouth and invigorate the palate). The pleasant surprise was a tomato coconut curry soup served in a demitasse cup. In a departure from the ordinary, for a nominal cost, the restaurant made a lasting positive impression. (And when restaurant guests are enticed to order a cup or bowl of the soup, the restaurant has actually increased its average check by providing a low-cost pleasant surprise.)

And not all pleasant surprises cost money. If a hotel guest is granted early access to or late departure from her room, the hotel has provided a pleasant surprise that costs nothing. Similarly, if a gate agent chooses to upgrade a passenger to an available economy-plus seat with more legroom, there is no hard cost to the airline, but a lasting positive impression has been made on the customer. At Disney's Wilderness Lodge, there is no additional cost for housekeepers to creatively reposition stuffed animals or Disney character dolls in rooms while their young masters are away enjoying the local attractions. When the children return at the end of the day, they are pleasantly surprised to find Winnie the Pooh playing cards with Tigger, Mickey Mouse watching TV, or Cinderella reading books with Donald Duck!

As illustrated by the Disney housekeepers, oftentimes, pleasant surprises are limited only by one's imagination and initiative. Years ago, I worked a full day in Washington, D.C., and then flew to Detroit for a presentation the following morning. I arrived late at the airport in Detroit. As I exited the terminal with my bags at around midnight, I encountered an immaculately dressed limousine driver whose Lincoln Town Car was spotless. I confirmed the fare to the Renaissance Center downtown, handed him my bags, and slid into the back seat through a door he held open.

When he returned to the driver's seat and began to pull away from the curb, he asked me what type of music I preferred. I told him that, at this late hour and with a thirty-minute ride ahead of us, I'd appreciate something mellow. He said, "Here, let me surprise you." And I nodded off to Tony Bennett singing "Because of You."

When we arrived at the hotel, the handoff to the staff was just as seamless and professional as my reception had been at the airport.

Naturally, I rewarded the driver's attention to detail and professionalism. Like most customers who are pleasantly surprised by the service they receive, I tipped more than I would have ordinarily. I also scheduled a return trip to the airport with him the following day. This demonstrates how pleasantly surprising customers not only benefits employees today but can lead to future business tomorrow.

There is even a science, known as Customer Lifetime Value (CLV), to determining the future spending a company can expect from its current customers. Roughly defined, CLV is the projected revenue that an average customer will generate during his lifetime. This is calculated using averaged variables such as sales per customer, purchase frequency, customer retention rate, profit margin, and time. It is well documented that the most effective ways to boost a customer's lifetime value are to increase his overall satisfaction and intent to repurchase. Bain & Company research reveals that a 5 percent increase in customer retention can increase profits by 25 to 95 percent. The same study found that it costs six to seven times more to gain a new customer than to keep an existing one.

And this is not just a theoretical platitude. It plays out in business every single day. For my fortieth birthday, my wife and I traveled to Las Vegas, where we met up with friends to relax by the pool, take in a show, and play a little blackjack. My wife had made reservations at Caesars Palace, which, ironically, was celebrating its fortieth anniversary. The front desk agent pointed this out as she handed me a room key containing a holograph with a black and white image of Caesars Palace in 1966; when rotated, it revealed a color image from the same vantage point in 2006. During our brief conversation, we joked about the theme song for my fortieth birthday celebration: Toby Keith's hit song "As Good as I Once Was."

Memorable room key in hand, we headed to our room in the newly opened Augustus Tower. It was then that I noticed our room number: 4089. When we reached our floor and exited the elevator, my wife took a picture of me next to the large number 40 designating our floor number. We then proceeded to our room, opened the door, and entered to find that our flat panel television set was playing a music video: Toby Keith's "As Good as I Once Was." Whether that was staged or just a bizarre coincidence, I was wowed! After we unpacked, Julie and I went downstairs to explore the sprawling facility. When we returned an hour later, there was a small gift and a handwritten note from the front desk agent wishing me a happy fortieth birthday and a pleasant stay.

So, how does this pleasant surprise relate to CLV? For one, it is clearly documented that there is a relationship between guest satisfaction and ancillary spending in a hotel setting. In one study, J.D. Power and Associates concluded that guests whose overall satisfaction was a 10 (or highly satisfied) on a ten-point scale spent an average of $14 more per day on supplemental goods and services (e.g., food and beverage outlets, gift shops, in-room movies) than guests who were less satisfied.

Here's how this dynamic played out at Caesars Palace: The first night of our stay, I canceled a reservation that we had made at a well-known sushi restaurant down the street in order to dine at the hotel's own sushi restaurant, Hyakumi Japanese Restaurant & Sushi Bar. And the payoff for Caesars Palace did not end there. A week later, in a note to Gary Selesner, the president of Caesars Palace, I committed to return to the hotel the next time I visited Las Vegas. Think about the number of hotels in Las Vegas that are attractions unto themselves. It would be perfectly natural to assume that guests would experiment by staying at a variety of competing properties, many of which are uniquely themed in order to differentiate themselves from competing hotels and casinos.

Even so, my commitment to Selesner was "to return to Caesars Palace the next time I visited Las Vegas." Notice that there are no qualifiers such as "if the location is convenient," "if the price is right," or "unless your competitors are offering free show tickets to reserve a room with them." My intent was to return to Caesars Palace. Period.

Provide Pleasant Surprises That Are Planned in Advance

While some pleasant surprises happen in the moment, others require careful advance planning on the part of service providers. As part of this planning, it is vital to check your assumptions at the door and be willing to reexamine conventional thinking and existing processes that may have provided steady, if not optimal, results in the past. Consider the process of conducting intercept surveys to obtain intelligence from consumers for marketing purposes.

How do you feel when you are unexpectedly approached by some-one, clipboard in hand, conducting a survey? Would you categorize this as a pleasant or an unpleasant surprise? Based on average participation rates from typical intercept surveys, most people would classify such surveys as an unpleasant surprise and would prefer to avoid them.

However, I worked with a client who reinvented the way in which these surveys were administered. As a result, participation rates doubled and the quantity and quality of feedback soared. This was accomplished by transforming a process that most people would describe as an unpleasant interruption into a pleasant surprise that participants would welcome.

CASE STUDY: TRANSFORMING THE INTERCEPT SURVEY WITH A PLEASANT SURPRISE

When traveling, motorists often stop at state visitor centers to take a break, verify directions, and learn more about local attractions. In the past, my client would dispatch surveyors to the state visitor centers to solicit feedback from visitors such as city of origin, final destination, length of stay, and frequency of visits. The participation rates and quality of feedback reflected the sentiment that most people have toward participating in such surveys.

Knowing this to be true, my client revisited the process and enhanced it by adding a pleasant surprise. Instead of approaching road-weary travelers with clipboards, her staff approached motorists with wash buckets and squeegees and offered to clean their windshields. As the surveyors removed the bug splatter that had accumulated over the past several hundred highway miles, a natural conversation evolved, guided by the surveyor, that elicited all the information that would ordinarily be acquired through a series of rehearsed questions.

Rather than being perceived by visitors as causing an interruption in their day that would cost them time, surveyors were seen as providing a pleasant surprise that would save visitors time. By planning in advance to provide visitors with a pleasant surprise, the state's tourism office better served its customers while at the same time improving the results of its marketing surveys.

As demonstrated by the squeegee-wielding surveyors, it is possible to provide pleasant surprises that, planned in advance, leave a positive lasting impression on customers. It is also possible (as you will read in the next example) to orchestrate pleasant surprises that leave customers speechless.

I was in New York City two weeks before my tenth wedding anniversary. One afternoon, I stopped by the Tiffany & Co. flagship store on 5th Avenue to look at anniversary rings. A thoughtful representative showed me several rings as he explained some of the nuances of color, cut, clarity, and carat weight.

The rings looked magnificent beneath the showroom lights. Of the half dozen or so rings that I looked at, there was one that I kept going back to. The salesman noticed it too. And, of course, that ring cost 25 percent more than the others. After about thirty minutes together, I thanked him for his time and told him that I wouldn't be buying the ring today. I mentioned that I had an appointment in two days with a representative at Tiffany's Denver location. He congratulated me on my upcoming anniversary and wished me luck in finding the perfect ring.

Two days later, I went to the Denver location of Tiffany & Co. for my appointment. The sales representative brought me into a private room to show me a set of anniversary rings that she had selected based on the criteria we had discussed. As she revealed each successive ring, she would say something like, "Now, this ring combines the color you are hoping for with the mounting we talked about."

After introducing several rings in this way, she produced the final ring, saying, "Now, this is the ring that you were especially taken by at the 5th Avenue store on Tuesday."

I was stunned! I said something like, "Huh? What? How did you . . . ?"

She sensed my astonishment, smiled, and then explained that she had received a call shortly after I had left the 5th Avenue store. In cooperation with the salesman I had met in New York, she had made arrangements for the ring to be shipped overnight to Denver in time for my appointment.

The two sales representatives had worked together to deliver customer service that was completely beyond the realm of customer expectation. I had no reason to expect that the ring I had looked at in New York on Tuesday would be among the options made available to me in Denver on Thursday.

Does this level of customer service influence sales? Guess which ring I bought?

Later, I wrote to the president of Tiffany & Co. about his employees' legendary customer service and committed to "never purchase a significant piece of jewelry from a jeweler other than Tiffany & Co." After customers make such a commitment, there is no coupon or incentive program out there that is strong enough to lure them (and their future spending) away.

Provide Pleasant Surprises as Follow-Up

Another way pleasant surprises can be used to make lasting positive impressions, forge relationships, and cement loyalty is by providing them as follow-up to an experience that a customer had with you or your organization. These pleasant surprises can be either scheduled or spontaneous. Scheduled follow-up is beneficial because it tends to occur consistently, whereas spontaneous follow-up is less reliable and often at the mercy of peoples' schedules.

Allstate Insurance schedules pleasant surprises as follow-up to policyholders who have demonstrated that they are safe drivers. For every six months of accident-free driving, policyholders can earn a Safe Driving Bonus® check for up to 5 percent of their auto insurance premiums.

Follow-up can also be spontaneous. Whenever people take the time to write thank-you notes to prospects, clients, or vendors they have dealt with, it shows that they understand the value of showing gratitude and maintaining relationships. Too often, busy professionals become, as author Stephen Covey observed, "constantly caught up in the thick of thin things." As a result, their good intentions to follow up fall by the wayside as they scramble to meet their busy schedule demands.

The reason people tend to be so impressed when others actually *do* follow up after the phone call, meeting, or sale is because most people don't follow up. If you are looking for a way to differentiate yourself or your organization, commit to providing pleasant surprises as follow-up.

I once exchanged business cards with a Riedel Crystal representative at an event in New York City. Although I did not expect to hear back from him, about a week later, I received a pair of Riedel O wine tumblers in the mail along with a nice note. Since that time, every piece of wine glassware I've purchased, without exception, has been made by Riedel Crystal. Although the Riedel representative I met made a fine impression at the time, his follow-up gesture solidified my commitment to the Riedel brand.

By listening to clients over the years, I've detected interests and priorities that have influenced my follow-up with them. One client mentioned that she purchased pins while traveling to add to her grandson's pin collection. Recalling our conversation, I bought a Colorado pin at the Denver International Airport and mailed it to her with a brief note. She let me know afterward that she was very touched by the gesture and the fact that I had remembered her comment about her grandson's collection.

Another time, I was having lunch with two international clients during a business trip. One revealed that she was challenged to create memorable slides using presentation software. The other revealed how much she enjoyed the cookies from a particular hotel company based in the United States, describing them in detail. After I returned home, I mailed the first client a copy of the book *Presentation Zen* by Garr Reynolds, and I sent the second client a box of cookies that were special-ordered to match her description of the hotel's cookies. Thank-you notes are always welcomed, but when you can take it one step further by sending an appropriate gift tailored to customers' expressed interests, it makes even more of an impact.

Just two weeks prior to writing this chapter, I met a young entrepreneur who had just opened his second coffee shop in Castle Rock, Colorado. I noticed that his store offered loyalty punch cards that would enable customers, after nine punches, to get their tenth cup of coffee free of charge. This brought to mind a study I had read about the tendency of consumers to redeem their loyalty punch cards at a higher rate when they receive a one-punch head start upon receipt of the card. I asked him if he was aware of the study. Intrigued, he said, "No, but I'm interested in reading it. What publication was it in?"

At the time I couldn't recall where I had seen the study, so I took his card and said I'd confirm the source and follow up with him afterward. Within a day or two, I located the study in the book *Switch* by Chip Heath and Dan Heath. Rather than scanning and e-mailing him the excerpt from the book, I purchased and shipped a copy to him with a short note encouraging the success of his coffee shops.

I have no illusions that the managing partner of a fledgling two-store chain of coffee shops will retain my services anytime soon. However, he might subscribe to my blog feed or refer me to a friend who is a better fit for my services. Perhaps he is a member of an association that polls its members for topic and speaker suggestions for its annual conference.

It's nice when you are rewarded with immediate sales for providing pleasant surprises as follow-up, but that's not why you do it. You do these things because you genuinely care about and are sincerely interested in others. Over time, customers (or prospective customers) will detect your sincerity, and this may factor into their decision-making process when it is time to buy. And if they don't choose your product or service right away, that's okay because you are in it for the long term, right? Besides, at one time, Starbucks operated only two locations in Seattle.

· · ·

Throughout this book, I've repeated the mantra that there is no additional cost to provide exceptional customer service. In this chapter, however, there are examples of providing pleasant surprises for which there are costs. For instance, there is a cost for the thirteenth pastry in a baker's dozen. There is a cost to provide a complimentary chef's taste. And there was a cost when the diamond salesman at Tiffany & Co. arranged to have the anniversary ring express mailed from New York City to Denver. Even so, these costs are negligible when compared to the lifetime value of a customer.

A study by the University of Connecticut calculated the lifetime value of an average supermarket customer to be $250,000. It makes a supermarket cashier's decision to refuse an expired rain check for a 99¢ can of tuna look a little ridiculous, doesn't it? It also validates a store manager's decision to refund $40 spent on fresh Atlantic salmon that the customer found to be unsatisfactory, with or without physical evidence.

Companies and employees who stingily manage the customer experience, for example when they choose to refuse to judiciously extend

expiration dates, deny refund requests that are outside the norm, or refuse to pleasantly surprise customers in other ways, sacrifice long-term
gain in their nearsighted pursuit of short-term profits.

Zappos is a company that has earned a reputation for extending lib-
eral return policies, expediting shipping at no additional cost to the customer, and providing other pleasant surprises to its legion of loyal customers. Tony Hsieh, the CEO of Zappos, justifies these customer-centric
practices, saying, "We actually take a lot of the money that we would
have normally spent on paid advertising and put it back into customer
experience. We've always stuck with customer service, even when it was
not a sexy thing to do." As a result, 75 percent of Zappos' sales come from
repeat customers who are delighted with its product and service quality.

As illustrated throughout this chapter, providing pleasant surprises
illustrates three truths of exceptional customer service:

1. It reflects the essence—the most critical aspect, the highest priority—of every service industry employee's job role.
2. It is always voluntary. An employee *chooses* to provide pleasant
   surprises.
3. There is little or no additional cost to provide pleasant surprises.

Consider the job role of the housekeepers at Disney's Wilderness
Lodge. Like every housekeeper's job role, it is made up of two parts:
job function and job essence. When housekeepers vacuum guest rooms
or change bedding, they are executing job functions by performing duties associated with their job roles. But when they creatively reposition
children's dolls, stuffed animals, or Disney character dolls to be reading
books or playing cards, housekeepers are displaying job essence by providing pleasant surprises to children upon their return from a day at the
theme park.

Housekeepers are *required* to vacuum guest rooms and change bedding. But their decisions to pleasantly surprise young hotel guests by
arranging their dolls in a variety of amusing poses are *voluntary*. They
don't have to provide pleasant surprises to capture the imagination of
children. Most housekeepers don't.

How much does it cost for the Disney housekeepers to provide pleasant surprises like these? *There is no additional cost.* Staging stuffed animals to the delight of children is free!

Most of the time, the customer service quality that consumers receive from frontline employees is pretty unremarkable. As employees myopically focus on executing job functions, interactions with customers become transactional and outcomes are predictable as each customer is treated like the last customer. In such work environments, employees unwittingly forfeit opportunities to showcase their own unique style and flair. And customers are left with experiences that they would describe as bland and uneventful.

Surprises, whether pleasant or unpleasant, disrupt the monotony, increase alertness, and narrow focus. In other words, surprises get customers' attention and tend to be the events that make the most significant impressions. Customers don't remember their interactions with employees; they remember *moments* within their interactions with employees. It may be the moment a server pleasantly surprises a restaurant guest with a complimentary chef's taste or the moment a policyholder receives an unexpected rebate check in the mail.

Opportunity lies in providing the unexpected, the pleasant surprises that make lasting positive impressions on your customers. In order to stand out from the ordinary, companies and employees should identify lagniappes to provide as part of their service offerings. These "little extras" reinforce customers' perception of value for the price paid. Employees must also be intentional about providing pleasant surprises in the moment, taking steps to provide pleasant surprises that are planned in advance, and providing pleasant surprises as follow-up. Doing so will contribute to the positive lasting impressions required to raise customers' service experiences from ordinary to extraordinary.

GETTING FROM ORDINARY TO EXTRAORDINARY

- Surprise is an emotion whose function is to increase alertness and narrow focus. By challenging customers' assumptions and exceeding their expectations, powerful, indelible memories are created.

- Providing a lagniappe—something that is added—or other little extras has the potential to pleasantly surprise customers while adding value for the price paid.
- Providing a pleasant surprise in the moment can disrupt the monotony of a routine transaction, making employees' jobs more satisfying and customers' experiences more memorable.
- Customer Lifetime Value (CLV) is the projected revenue that an average customer will generate during her lifetime. This is calculated using averaged variables such as sales per customer, purchase frequency, customer retention rate, profit margin, and time.
- When providing pleasant surprises that are planned in advance, it is vital to check your assumptions at the door and be willing to reexamine conventional thinking and existing processes that may have provided steady, if not optimal, results in the past.
- Providing pleasant surprises, scheduled or spontaneous, as follow-up to experiences that customers had with you or your organization, can make lasting positive impressions, forge relationships, and cement loyalty.
- Companies and employees who stingily manage the customer experience by choosing to refuse to judiciously extend expiration dates, deny refund requests that are outside the norm, or refuse to pleasantly surprise customers in other ways sacrifice long-term gain in their nearsighted pursuit of short-term profits.
- Customers don't remember their interactions with employees; they remember *moments* within their interactions with employees.
- Providing pleasant surprises reflects the essence—the most critical aspect, the highest priority—of every service industry employee's job role.
- Providing pleasant surprises is always voluntary. An employee *chooses* to provide pleasant surprises.
- There is little or no additional cost to provide pleasant surprises. Any cost that may be incurred is negligible when compared to the lifetime value of a customer.

Applying Pleasant Surprises

In the space provided, record examples of how you can apply concepts from the chapter to raise customer service quality that you deliver or influence from ordinary to extraordinary!

ORDINARY	EXTRAORDINARY
Interrupt motorists by confronting them with a clipboard, pen, and questionnaire while conducting intercept surveys to gain valuable insight into their travel plans.	Pleasantly surprise motorists by approaching them with a wash bucket, squeegee, and informal questions to gain valuable insight into their travel plans.

8

Deliver Service Heroics

Martin Luther King, Jr., said, "Everyone has the power for greatness, not for fame, but greatness, because greatness is determined by service."

To deliver service heroics is to go the extra mile, to go above and beyond what a customer might expect given the employee's job role. In short, it's to deliver greatness. Delivering greatness doesn't come easy, and it doesn't happen every day. Fortunately, it's also rarely required of an employee. It's the exception rather than the rule. But when the situation calls for it and an employee goes out of her way to serve a customer, it makes a lasting positive impression that reaffirms the customer's importance and reinforces the relationship.

Some employees have a penchant for delivering service heroics that become the subject of many positive customer testimonials and, in rare cases, company lore. Do you recall the Tiffany & Co. story from the previous chapter, where the sales representatives from New York City and Denver partnered to plan a pleasant surprise for me while I shopped for an anniversary ring? That was pretty remarkable, wasn't it? And if the story ended there, it would be impressive by itself—but the story did not end there.

After I purchased the ring at Tiffany's Denver location, it required sizing, and it would not be available until the following day. Since my wife and I were planning to spend our anniversary at the Broadmoor Hotel in Colorado Springs, about an hour and a half from our home in southeast Denver, I made arrangements for the ring to be shipped from the store to the hotel's food and beverage director. He and I had schemed to incorporate the ring into the dessert presentation following our anniversary dinner.

As it happened, Denver was hit by a snowstorm the morning of our anniversary, and we cancelled our plans to drive to Colorado Springs. Meanwhile, the ring had already been shipped and was in the process of being delivered to the hotel by United Parcel Service.

I contacted the sales rep at the Tiffany store with my dilemma, and she assured me that she would take care of it. What happened next was legendary. The store arranged for one of its intrepid security guards to drive two hours to Colorado Springs, where he located the UPS truck transporting the ring, provided the paperwork necessary to claim the package, and then drove the ring another hour and a half to my house.

I've heard similar testimonials from others when presenting customer service training around the country. Without exception, the one element that each of these stories has in common is the customer's resulting unconditional loyalty to the company involved.

Two Types of Service Heroics

There are two types of service heroics. There are *no-fault service heroics* that are delivered to customers or prospective customers in response to situational opportunities for which there is no fault of the company or service provider and no expectation by the customer. And there are *at-fault service heroics* that are delivered to customers or prospective customers in reaction to problems caused by the company or service provider for which a remedy is expected by the customer.

Service heroics are most often born out of crisis in reaction to a setback experienced by a customer. However, there are also times when employees display service heroics by seizing opportunities to delight customers, even though no problem exists (as demonstrated by the New York City Tiffany & Co. sales representative discussed in Chapter 7). Regardless of the circumstances, delivering service heroics requires that employees embrace these situations as opportunities rather than seeing them as interruptions or hassles that they would prefer to avoid.

No-Fault Service Heroics

As illustrated by the Tiffany & Co. illustration, there are opportunities to go the extra mile for customers in situations where the company is not at fault and there is no customer expectation of service heroics. Tiffany fulfilled its responsibility when it shipped the ring as requested to the Broadmoor Hotel. However, it was not Tiffany's responsibility to send an employee two hours south in snowy weather to track down the UPS truck carrying the ring, obtain the package, and then drive another ninety minutes to hand-deliver it to me at my home. And I certainly did not expect the company to do so.

All three Tiffany & Co. employees I dealt with had one quality in common, without which I guarantee I would not have purchased the ring and certainly would not have received it in time to present to my wife on our anniversary. That quality is initiative.

In Chapter 2, I wrote that service is a verb. That's true, isn't it? Delivering exceptional customer service in general requires action on the part of the service provider. The opposite of action is inaction or indifference. Too often, when employees are presented with an opportunity to deliver service heroics and make a lasting positive impression on a customer, they instead choose to do nothing. After all, when they are being paid by the hour, apathetic employees are paid the same as those who demonstrate initiative. Many listless employees justify their inaction by saying things like, "We can't control the weather" or "It's not our responsibility" or "We did our job. It's his problem now."

Here's an example of another employee who chose action over inaction.

CASE STUDY: A RED ROBIN TEAM MEMBER
DELIVERS SERVICE HEROICS

A family of four dined at Red Robin Gourmet Burgers in Aurora, Colorado, before heading to a nearby Verizon Wireless Store. There, the youngest boy, an eighth grader, planned to preorder an iPhone 5 with money he had saved. After waiting in line and finally making his way to the register to reserve the phone, the boy realized that his wallet containing his savings of $320 was missing.

Frantic, his mother phoned the restaurant to see whether anyone had turned in a wallet. A Red Robin team member searched throughout the section of the restaurant where the family had been seated and located the wallet. But, to the family's dismay, all of the cash had been removed.

The family returned to the restaurant to pick up the empty wallet, and the server met the boy whose savings had been stolen. With tears in his eyes, the boy recounted his sense of helplessness when he realized that he had lost his wallet. The boy's parents left their home telephone number on the off-chance that someone turned in the money.

Later that night, the Red Robin server shared the story with his parents and said that he would like to rally other team members at the restaurant to see if they could raise money to offset some of the boy's loss. His father reached into his wallet, removed a bill, and said, "Here's $20 to start your fund."

The next day at work, the server shared the story with his coworkers. Over the course of the day, he collected donations from them. That afternoon, after consulting his manager, the server phoned the boy's home, spoke with his mother, and invited the entire family back to Red Robin that evening as his guests for dinner. When they arrived, he and his coworkers presented the boy with a card of encouragement signed by the staff, and $320—the exact amount missing from his wallet.

Red Robin encourages its team members to perform Unbridled Acts® of service, defined on its website as "random acts of kindness" that team members bestow on restaurant guests and other team members. Clearly, the Red Robin server here demonstrated that this is much more than a corporation's empty customer service platitude. Even though the restaurant was not at fault and the customer had no expectation of any action on the server's part, the server delivered service heroics to resolve the issue. It is a way of doing business and a true testament to Red Robin's amazing service culture and the care expressed for its customers.

At-Fault Service Heroics

Whereas no-fault service heroics are delivered by employees who are *not* responsible for rectifying the situation, at-fault service heroics are predicated on problems for which the company or service provider *is* responsible.

Throughout this book, I've been repeating that exceptional customer service costs no more to deliver than average customer service. And while it's possible to deliver service heroics without incurring extra costs, in cases of at-fault service heroics, you might have to get your checkbook out.

My in-laws recently launched a Sunday brunch at their steakhouse. Since they had not advertised the brunch beyond a handful of social media postings, they did not expect a large turnout, and their staffing, food inventories, and kitchen preparations reflected this. Within the first hour, though, all of the available cold-prep items had been exhausted, and orders were taking sixty minutes or more to fill. In order to calm restive guests, my father-in-law, Ed, went from table to table comping meals, providing complimentary meal certificates for use in the future, and encouraging guests to order any bottle of wine they wished from the menu, free of charge, including expensive Cabernets from Silver Oak, Jordan, and Cakebread Cellars.

When Ed and I chatted about this later, he said that although decisions like these are expensive, he received numerous positive comments on the food quality (when it eventually arrived at the tables) and the attitude of the wait staff (even though they were "in the weeds" most of the afternoon). He said that in lieu of paying for their meals, many guests left tips of 50 to 100 percent, thanking him for his generosity and promising to return with friends in the near future. Ed understands that the success of his restaurant does not hinge on its profitability on any given Sunday. It hinges on the lifetime value of a delighted customer.

I'd like to make a distinction here between *service recovery protocol*, which refers to scripted actions designed to address or remedy service failures, and at-fault service heroics. Even companies with poor customer service reputations have specific service recovery protocols in place. For example, when airlines and hotels overbook available inventory of airline seats and hotel rooms, employees often follow a documented policy or procedure to compensate affected customers for the service failure. An airline might provide a combination of meal vouchers, transportation reimbursement, lodging, or airfare vouchers. Hotels might cover similar costs for guests who are "walked" to different hotels and continue to cover lodging expenses when they return to the offending hotel as accommodations become available.

So, it's possible to execute service recovery protocol without delivering at-fault service heroics. Executing protocol is a job function (a task associated with a job role) that is mandated by the employer. It's what an employee is paid to do. There's nothing remarkable about it. At-fault service heroics, however, reflect job essence (an employee's highest priority at work) that is voluntary and for which the employee is not paid a premium. Employees' hourly wage rates are constant and do not fluctuate depending on whether they execute ordinary protocol or go above and beyond by delivering service heroics.

The following example illustrates the difference between following standard service recovery protocol that treats each customer like the last customer and delivering exceptional at-fault service heroics.

A couple of years ago, I brought my car into the Cadillac dealership for maintenance. The dealership offers both a waiting area and a shuttle service to take you to local destinations while your vehicle is being serviced.

While leaving my keys with the service department, I inquired about the shuttle driver. I was told that he was currently off-site and would return in the next fifteen minutes or so. I then asked the rep if he would have the driver locate me in the waiting area when he returned so that I could run a local errand while my car was being serviced.

The rep agreed, made note of my name and cell phone number, and assured me that it would be no more than fifteen minutes. While I was sitting in the waiting area, a client called on my cell phone. I took the call and moved to a quiet corner of the waiting area to talk. Within five minutes or so, the shuttle driver appeared and called out my name. I motioned to the driver that I was on the phone and would be a few minutes.

The driver left the area, returning a few minutes later. As I was listening to my client and taking notes in my planner, the driver walked toward me, pointed to his watch, motioned for me to wind things up, and said, "I've got places to go."

Stunned by his actions, I instructed him not to wait for me and said that I would just take the next available shuttle. Clearly annoyed, he let out an audible sigh, turned, and walked away. After my call ended, I approached the dealership's general manager and we sat together briefly in his office. I shared what had happened, recognizing my contribution to the misunderstanding.

I realize that conflict doesn't occur in a vacuum. Conflict is the result of a failure to meet expectations—and I clearly had not met the shuttle driver's expectations. After all, I had requested the shuttle service and then wasn't available when the driver returned. Even so, I told the GM that the driver's behavior made me feel devalued as a customer. (His dealership spends a lot of money to evoke certain feelings from its customers, and I'm quite certain "devalued" isn't one of them.)

What the GM did next cemented my loyalty to his dealership and the Cadillac brand. He said, "Here, take my car," as he handed me the key to a brand new white Cadillac CTS in the parking lot.

As we walked from his office to the showroom, he apologized on behalf of the shuttle driver, thanked me for my business, and said, "Take as long as you need. I'm here until 7 o'clock." His overture demonstrates the compassion and creativity that goes into providing service heroics that you do not find in typical service recovery protocol.

The next section introduces the fundamental truths of heroic problem resolution that will lay the foundation for employees to constructively uncover and resolve legitimate problems experienced by customers.

How to Deliver Heroic Service to Solve Customers' Problems

Whether or not a company or employee is at fault, it is important to view problems experienced by customers as opportunities and to see customers as partners rather than adversaries. Of course, the best way to deal with problems that you have caused for your customers is to avoid causing them in the first place. It is always preferable to have adequate staffing and food inventories if you run a restaurant, to honor reservations if you operate an airline or hotel, and to employ courteous shuttle drivers if you manage a car dealership. But alas, we live and work in a world made up of imperfect people and flawed processes.

For that reason, it is important that employees acknowledge the following fundamental truths of heroic problem resolution: the customer's problem is their problem, "discerning" customers are not "difficult," exceptions require exceptional customer service, and individual customers are irreplaceable.

Treat Your Customer's Problem as Your Problem

Some companies and employees treat a customer's problem as though it's only the customer's problem. It makes me want to ask them, "Why isn't this problem as important to you as it is to me?"

Recently, a design consultant from a window blinds company came to my home to measure two windows for replacement blinds and valances. During the visit, I inquired about ordering replacement cord condensers (the small plastic pieces that bind the ends of the blind cords) because, after ten years and four kids, several cord condensers throughout the house were missing.

She replied, "You could call someone else and get those."

Surprised by her response, I said, "I'm confused. You represent a window blinds company. Whom else should I call to order replacement window blinds cord condensers?"

In that moment, it was as if the irony of her initial reply dawned on her. She relented, saying that she would see what she could do. But why did it take me having to challenge her apparent lack of initiative to achieve a positive result?

I had a similar experience last spring with my lawn service. After my lawn had been aerated and fertilized, I noticed yellow grass forming along the eastern perimeter of the front yard. My initial thought was that the lawn service had inadvertently oversprayed grass killer while treating the rock landscaping that borders the lawn. I called and asked if a rep could come out and take a look at it.

A couple days later, a tech stopped by to examine the grass and told me I had lawn mites. He suggested I rake the yellow areas to remove the dead layer of grass. As he prepared to leave, I asked, "Is there something you can do to eliminate the lawn mites?" He said that he would add it to my next service ticket but, in the meantime, I should reseed or resod the areas of the lawn that had been damaged.

Later, I went to the lawn service's website and found an entire page devoted to the detection and treatment of lawn mites. I contacted the same service tech who had diagnosed the problem and asked why— since his company dedicates an entire web page to the detection and treatment of lawn mites—this issue had not been addressed in the preventative maintenance done last fall or earlier this spring. And why, I asked, was it my responsibility—when his company had twice serviced my lawn in the previous thirty days—to identify the problem, schedule a tech inspection, and replace the affected areas of grass, when I had retained a lawn service to ensure the health of my lawn?

I told him, "I think our goals are the same: a green lawn. I'm writing checks and watering regularly, but I expect you to manage the rest. Even if lawn mites were beyond the scope of our service agreement, I would expect your advice regarding treatment, even if additional charges apply, because we both want a green lawn, right? Does this sound reasonable to you?"

To his credit, the service tech did not become defensive. He agreed that my expectations were reasonable, accepted responsibility, and returned the following day to repair the damaged areas of the lawn.

When your customers have a problem, you have a problem. Rather than overlooking the issue or passing the buck to customers, accept personal responsibility and express genuine interest in resolving the problem quickly.

Understand That "Discerning" Customers Are Not "Difficult" Customers

From time to time, seminar participants ask me, "What's the best way to deal with difficult customers?"

My standard answer is: "They're only difficult if you've labeled them that way." I prefer the adjective "discerning" in place of "difficult." Consider the definitions of each:

Discerning: noting differences or distinctions; exhibiting keen insight and good judgment; perceptive
Difficult: hard to please or satisfy

Oftentimes, when customers complain, it's because their expectations were not met. This is not an indication that they are hard to please. It's a signal that they have noted a difference between what they originally expected and what they ultimately received.

Too often, employees go on the defensive in these situations. You can see it in their faces and their body movements. Their smiles fade and they may fold their arms. As they begin to speak, the tone of their voice becomes a bit more serious—even condescending—as they retreat to the safety of "policy" and "terms and conditions."

I once observed a visibly disappointed customer at Office Depot. He was upset because, in the middle of processing his order, an employee in the print center had left for several minutes to assist a customer in another part of the store. Eventually, he was approached by a store supervisor.

This customer wasn't hard to please. He simply noted a difference between what he originally expected (timely fulfillment of his print order) and what he ultimately received (an unexpected delay without explanation).

I observe these confrontations on occasion and am always pleased when employees are willing to let the customer vent and they take the time to really listen for understanding of the customer's problem. More often than not, customers simply want to be heard and have their complaints be acknowledged and validated.

A great technique for employees to demonstrate that they fully understand the customer's complaint is to paraphrase (not parrot) the facts and feelings they heard while the customer vented. An apology may also be in order, whether or not the employee was at fault.

For example, the Office Depot supervisor who approached the customer could respond, "I apologize that you had to wait while Mark assisted another customer. It's frustrating when there's no communication about how long the wait will be." The supervisor could then choose to complete the print job personally and, perhaps, discount the order to compensate for the unexpected delay.

Upon completion, the supervisor should reinforce her earlier apology and make the customer aware of the discount applied to the order. Then, she should express appreciation for the feedback by saying something like, "My name's Laura. I'm a supervisor and I'll share your experience with the entire team in order to improve our responsiveness and communication in the future."

While it's true that some customers are more discerning than others, this does not mean these customers are "difficult." These customers do, however, present unique opportunities for employees to heighten their sense of urgency, attention to detail, and follow-up in the pursuit of exceptional customer service.

Handle Exceptional Situations with Exceptional Customer Service

Have you ever noticed the tendency of frontline employees to become defensive—even surly—when you bring a problem or misunderstanding to their attention? Unless your business has chronic, unresolved issues (in which case, you may want to update your résumé), problems and misunderstandings are *exceptions*. By definition, exceptions do not conform to the general rule. This makes them infrequent. That's why they are exceptions.

When exceptions occur in your place of business, how are they typically handled?

In many cases, exceptions are customer dilemmas, misunderstand-ings, or unmet expectations that, when brought to the attention of front-line employees, create a palpable communication barrier that neutral-izes employees' smiles, eye contact, and enthusiasm to serve. It's as if a customer's dilemma, when expressed, drives a wedge between him and the employee. Then, instead of seeing the situation as an opportunity to serve, many employees recoil and judge the customer as being difficult or misinformed.

Consider the couple who enter a popular restaurant on a Friday evening without a reservation. Does the hostess work her magic to ac-commodate them, or is she dismissive because of their nonconformance, presumption, and naivety? ("Can you imagine? Showing up *here*, on a *Friday* night, *without* a reservation, *expecting* an open table? The *nerve* of some people!")

I recently arrived at Denver International Airport and stopped by Heidi's Brooklyn Deli for a sandwich. As I approached the counter, I heard the customer ahead of me ask if the bread for his sandwich could be sliced thinner than the pre-sliced bread that was visible at the coun-ter. (Ordinarily, the employees at Heidi's slice the sandwich bread off the fresh-baked loaves when preparing the customer's order. However, at the airport location, because of the volume of customers, the bread is sliced in advance and stored in clear plastic tubs.) The pre-sliced bread behind the counter was quite thick. As I learned, the customer had re-cently been diagnosed with TMJ syndrome, which causes chronic pain that restricts how wide he could comfortably open his mouth.

The employee responded that the bread had been pre-sliced and could not be sliced thinner. The customer moved down toward the reg-ister to order just a drink and a bag of chips.

Meanwhile, I noticed that in the open kitchen to the left, there were dozens of loaves of bread stored on racks. I asked the employee if one of those loaves could be used to accommodate the customer who required thinner slices. At first she said no because, according to her, the auto-mated bread slicer produced slices of a standard thickness.

Then I asked her if she had a bread knife behind the counter. At this point, she appeared to connect the dots and said that she might be able to honor the customer's request after all.

The customer overheard our conversation. He approached me and said, "Thank you. Now I can order a sandwich. By the way," he asked as he winked, "what's good here besides the service?"

How many customers do you think will request thinner slices of bread at the Denver International Airport location of Heidi's today? Two? Three? Four? I'm not sure, but I can say this with certainty: These requests will be infrequent. They will be exceptions. And exceptions require exceptional customer service.

Most employees don't choose to deliver poor customer service; they just don't choose to deliver exceptional customer service. Instead, most service providers are content to simply occupy customer service job roles and execute a set of mandated job functions, blissfully unaware of the opportunities they forfeit daily to take initiative in the moment of choice to delight their customers.

Sometimes, customer requests that are outside the norm require a bit more initiative and creativity than simply using a knife to accommodate a customer's request for thinner slices of bread. For instance, how would most front desk agents respond if, during check-in, a hotel guest requests that the *New York Times* be delivered to her room in the morning but the only newspapers offered are the local paper, the *Wall Street Journal*, and *USA TODAY*?

Here are some anticipated responses:

* "We don't have the *New York Times*. You're in Seattle."
* "Sorry. We only have the local paper, the *Wall Street Journal*, and *USA TODAY*."
* "We don't offer the *New York Times* but I know they carry it at the Starbucks across the street."

Instead of these responses, if you know it's possible to get the *New York Times*, why not list the papers offered and then say, "Let me see what I can do." After all, it's not like the guest is asking for the *Frankfurter Allgemeine Zeitung*—although the very best employees will find that newspaper too.

When customers don't have a strong preference, they're likely to say something like, "Oh, it's no big deal. I read the *New York Times* every day. *USA TODAY* will be fine." If you sense otherwise, however, then this may be an opportunity to shine.

If you're working the early shift tomorrow, why not swing by Starbucks on your way to work and then WOW the guest by placing the paper outside her room—perhaps with a personalized sticky note. And if you're not working the early shift, then make arrangements with a manager or another employee who does work the early shift. By doing so, you make everyone's job more interesting and make a lasting positive impression on the guest in the process!

Some employees might say, "If you do it for *one* guest, now you have to do it for *every* guest." That's ridiculous. It's an excuse used by average employees to justify average customer service. It's a rationale used by those who either don't want to go out of their way or simply prefer the predictable routine of treating each customer like the last customer, neither of which inspires loyal customers who will brag about you.

Accommodating customer preferences is only as difficult as employees make it. When employees learn of a unique preference from a customer, they should project through their body language and vocal tone that they consider the request to be reasonable and that, if there is a practical way to do so, they will make it happen.

That being said, reacting to exceptions as the rule is unsustainable. In other words, if Heidi's employees find themselves having to regularly accommodate customer requests for thinner bread slices, or if front desk agents are consistently reacting to guest requests for the *New York Times*, then these businesses must revisit and update the related service models. Doing so allows employees to consistently meet the needs of customers without having to constantly react to, or worse, say no to these types of requests.

In the outstanding book *Uncommon Service* by Frances Frei and Anne Morriss, the authors advise readers to "be the anti-hero." The point they are making is that if companies rely on a few extraordinary employees to react tirelessly to systemic flaws in product and service quality in order to placate customers, then it's only a matter of time before these chronic service recovery efforts lead to employee dissatisfaction, burnout, and turnover. As the authors rightly caution, "The cape starts to feel heavy when it's overused."

Recognize That Individual Customers Are Irreplaceable

Earlier this month during a presentation, a participant posed the following question: "What difference does it make if one customer leaves dissatisfied when there's a line of customers waiting to take his place?"

Having worked in high-volume environments like New York City and Orlando, Florida, I've detected this sentiment and even heard the same question from frontline employees who took for granted that there would always be a line of customers waiting to hand over their money.

Some employees are fortunate to work in bustling environments where demand is strong and customer volume is high. Such operations often charge price premiums and realize solid profits. Because their products or services are in demand and the operations are profitable, employees in these establishments may rationalize that if they lose a dissatisfied customer, they make up for the lost revenue with the next customer (or ten customers) in line.

This rationale is flawed, fuels arrogance, and produces attitudes of indifference toward customers and entitlement to their spending. What these employees fail to recognize is that, regardless of demand, *individual customers are irreplaceable*. I first read this notion in the outstanding book *Exceptional Service, Exceptional Profit* by Leonardo Inghilleri and Micah Solomon.

Conventional thinking about customer retention is that customers are replaceable. That is, when one customer leaves, another customer takes her place. But Inghilleri and Solomon are not talking about the anonymous masses. They are talking about the dismissed couple who was admonished by the condescending hostess because they lacked the foresight to reserve a table in advance at a popular restaurant. And they are talking about the frustrated moviegoer who, after waiting a full five minutes in a line that failed to move, chose to skip the buttered popcorn and Coke so he wouldn't miss the dramatic opening scene of the film.

If the dismissed couple and the frustrated moviegoer are not satisfied with their experiences, they may choose to defect to other restaurants and theaters in search of more respect, flexibility, efficiency, responsiveness, or a number of other factors. And because a majority of customers do not complain, you may never know that they left or why they left.

And here's the scary part: The admonished couple and the anonymous moviegoer are *irreplaceable*. When they decide to quit doing business with you, they mean it. So even if you attract a new customer's spending, you won't receive another nickel from these dissatisfied individual customers ever again.

Recognize that individual customers are *irreplaceable*. When they choose to defect, companies forfeit their lifetime contribution to the business, including future spending, feedback, and referrals.

. . .

As illustrated throughout this chapter, delivering service heroics illustrates three truths of exceptional customer service:

1. It reflects the essence—the most critical aspect, the highest priority—of every service industry employee's job role.
2. It is always voluntary. An employee *chooses* to deliver service heroics.
3. There is little or no additional cost to deliver service heroics.

Consider the job role of the Red Robin server we met earlier in the chapter. Like every restaurant server's job role, it is made up of two parts: job function and job essence. When servers answer questions about the menu or deliver food orders to the table, they are executing job functions by performing duties associated with their job roles. But when the server took the initiative to organize a collection on behalf of an eighth grader whose savings were stolen from his wallet, he displayed job essence by delivering service heroics.

Restaurant servers are *required* to answer questions about the menu and deliver food orders to the table. However, the server's decision to deliver service heroics by rallying coworkers to contribute funds to his cause was *voluntary*. He didn't have to organize the fundraiser. Most restaurant servers wouldn't.

How much did it cost Red Robin for their employee to deliver service heroics by organizing the fundraiser? *There was no additional cost.* Taking the initiative to reimburse a young boy for his lost savings is free!

Delivering service heroics is the exception rather than the rule.

Whereas opportunities abound to demonstrate many of the customer service behaviors presented in this book, delivering service heroics is situational. When the situation does present itself, whether or not the company or employee is at fault, it is important that employees reflect the fundamental truths of heroic problem resolution.

GETTING FROM ORDINARY TO EXTRAORDINARY

- To deliver service heroics is to go the extra mile, to go above and beyond what a customer might expect given the employee's job role.
- No-fault service heroics are delivered to customers or prospective customers in response to situational opportunities for which there is no fault of the company or service provider and no expectation by the customer.
- At-fault service heroics are delivered to customers or prospective customers in reaction to problems caused by the company or service provider for which a remedy is expected by the customer.
- Treat your customer's problem as your problem. Rather than overlooking the issue or passing the buck to customers, accept personal responsibility and express genuine interest in resolving the problem quickly.
- Understand that "discerning" customers are not "difficult" customers. Oftentimes, when customers complain, it's because their expectations were not met. This is not an indication that they are hard to please. It's a signal that they have noted a difference between what they originally expected and what they ultimately received.
- Handle exceptional situations with exceptional customer service. When problems or misunderstandings occur, instead of recoiling and judging customers as being difficult or misinformed, see the situation for what it is: an anomaly that creates an opportunity to provide exceptional customer service.
- Recognize that individual customers are *irreplaceable*. When they choose to defect, companies forfeit their lifetime contribution to the business, including future spending, feedback, and referrals.
- Delivering service heroics reflects the essence—the most critical aspect, the highest priority—of every service industry employee's job role.

- Delivering service heroics is always voluntary. An employee *chooses* to go above and beyond to serve his customers.
- There is little or no additional cost to deliver service heroics. And any cost that may be incurred is negligible when compared to the lifetime value of a customer.

Applying Service Heroics

In the space provided, record examples of how you can apply concepts from the chapter to raise customer service quality that you deliver or influence from ordinary to extraordinary!

ORDINARY	EXTRAORDINARY
Suggest that a customer rake and reseed areas of his lawn affected by lawn mites.	Send a service technician to the customer's home to rake and reseed the areas of his lawn affected by lawn mites.
●	●
●	●
●	●
●	●

Part Three

INCORPORATING JOB ESSENCE INTO JOB FUNCTION

9

From Ordinary to Extraordinary

To get from ordinary to extraordinary, you have to do something different. Business as usual produces the usual results: transactional customer service delivered by indifferent, uninspired employees. There are far too many companies with reputations for providing ordinary customer service (or worse) and far too many employees who are content to uphold the status quo, refusing to go out of their way in the service of others and treating each customer like the last customer.

In Chapter 1, I made the point that the reason you and I as customers inconsistently receive exceptional customer service is because it's voluntary. It's true. In order for anything to be made exceptional, it requires taking the initiative to do more than simply go through the motions. And this requires a deliberate choice. It is elective, optional, and discretionary. Employees don't have to make the choice to elevate an ordinary transaction to an extraordinary experience, and most don't.

Though business has its own set of complexities, customer service isn't one of them. Employees develop their own definitions of customer service and decide for themselves how they view customers: as honored contributors to the success of the enterprise, or as fickle adversaries who are just looking for the best deal. But most customer service employees have not made a conscious choice to provide exceptional service. As a result, they are indifferent toward both customer service and customers.

Why haven't they made a conscious choice? No one has asked them to. In most cases, no one has even brought it up. As a result, service employees go about their shifts tending to the mandatory job functions for which they are accountable but give little or no thought to the essence of their jobs, their highest priority at work—to create delighted customers.

Oftentimes, employees don't even recognize when they treat customers indifferently. Most would likely rate the quality of their personal customer service as excellent. Take, for example, the bellman we'll call "Phil" who appears in the following illustration. (Although the name "Phil" is fictitious, the story is quite true—and all too common.)

CASE STUDY: THE INDIFFERENT BELLMAN

A few summers ago, my family and I traveled to Lincoln, Nebraska, to attend a family reunion. While in Lincoln, we stayed at a full-service hotel downtown. When we arrived at the hotel, we unloaded several bags from our vehicle onto the sidewalk in front of the hotel. Minutes later, Phil passed by without saying a word and entered the main lobby from the sidewalk.

My wife and I fully expected that he was getting a luggage cart to assist us with our bags. When he did not return, I went inside the hotel and found Phil standing just inside the lobby. When I looked at him, he asked, "Can I help you with your bags?" I was already annoyed because I had to seek him out to provide assistance, even though he clearly saw our bags on the sidewalk.

Now that we were being helped, we no longer felt ignored, but we did feel as if Phil was treating us indifferently, as if we were "just another check-in." It's not that he did anything wrong during the remainder of the check-in process. He just missed several opportunities to anticipate our needs and make a lasting positive impression.

For instance, one of my boys complained about the weight of his backpack. Phil just stood there as I took the pack off my son's back and hung it on the luggage cart. A minute later, while I went back to the car to retrieve a cooler, my wife corralled the children in the lobby to take a group picture of them. She later commented that she wished she had asked Phil to take the picture so that she could have been included. This was another missed opportunity for Phil to display initiative by offering to take the photo.

When we arrived at our room, Phil simply offloaded the luggage near the door, accepted his tip, and bid us adieux with the transactional industry farewell, "Enjoy your stay."

Phil missed other cues that would have made the difference between an ordinary check-in process and an extraordinary service experience. Although a cooler, travel crib, and wine tote were all visible prompts, he appeared aloof from any customer service opportunities these items may have presented. In the first ten minutes after his departure, I got ice for the cooler, phoned housekeeping for a sheet to line the travel crib, and went in search of wine glasses.

With so many missed opportunities, the potential for an extraordinary customer-focused experience faded, and we were left with an ordinary and forgettable process-focused transaction. As happens far too often, many service providers are lulled into the monotony of processing "each customer like the last customer" and, in so doing, treating every customer like just another transaction. Or, in our case, "just another check-in."

Contrast Phil's ordinary customer service with the extraordinary customer service offered by tennis pro Matt Previdi, who was featured in Chapter 2. Matt demonstrated that service is a verb. As such, it requires action and effort. It must be demonstrated. Whereas Phil missed opportunities, Matt capitalized on them by expressing genuine interest in me and by displaying initiative, which may be the single most decisive attribute distinguishing extraordinary customer service from ordinary customer service. Because of his initiative, Matt literally *created* $111 in sales that did not even exist by influencing me to have three perfectly good sets of strings cut out of my rackets and replaced with strings by SOLINCO, the brand of string he was representing.

Some managers may say, "Well, if I had employees who were motivated and demonstrated initiative like Matt, then we would be able to offer extraordinary customer service too. But instead, I'm stuck with a lot of 'Phils' who are content to go through the motions and provide ordinary customer service."

First of all, there is no such thing as a lot of "Matts" or "Phils." There's only one Matt and only one Phil. Every individual employee is uniquely singular and, as such, has a different personality, style, and potential. By the time Matt or Phil show up in the employment office, their unique tendencies and attributes are pretty much baked. They are who they are. (While employee selection is beyond the scope of this book, employers who are renowned for their customer service quality invest heavily in predictive employee selection tools that screen for initiative and other traits that are complementary to superior customer service.)

Beyond selection, it's critical to recognize the influence of the organization, especially the immediate supervisor, in shaping the quality of customer service delivered by employees. This begins with understanding why ordinary customer service is so common and extraordinary customer service is so rare.

Why Ordinary Customer Service Is Common and Extraordinary Customer Service Is Rare

When is the last time you picked up your dry cleaning or deli sandwich and did not receive a bill? Now think about the last time you received service and did not get a smile. My hunch is that you have received many more bills for services rendered than you have received genuine smiles, eye contact, and enthusiasm in the voices of the employees who handed you the bills.

The reason for this is pretty clear. Protocol and processes are in place to predict reliable outcomes relative to job function. There is a process in place to open a checking account. There is a recognized process to conduct a seventy-five–point automotive safety check. There is a documented process followed to clean a hotel room. There is a sometimes protracted process to clear the security checkpoint at an airport. And there is most certainly a reliable process that produces your monthly electric bill.

It's no wonder that executing job functions produces such consistent outcomes. Employees are following a prescribed process. They are acutely aware of the related steps and sequence, which are usually documented in great detail. Employees have undergone training in order to properly execute the mandatory job functions outlined in the process. Expectations of success are clear, and employees may receive feedback on their performance and reinforcement through leadership's modeling.

An employee's tendency to demonstrate job essence, however, depends on the employee involved. This explains why, even in companies renowned for their customer service quality, it's still possible to receive disappointing customer service. Exceptional customer service hinges on the one-on-one interactions that customers have with service providers.

Whereas the duties or tasks associated with one's job role (job functions) are executed reliably *regardless of the employee involved*, exceptional customer service (job essence) is demonstrated inconsistently *because of the employee involved*.

Why Ordinary Customer Service Is Common

There is rarely a hiccup when a bank representative opens a checking account with a new customer. The seventy-five–point automotive safety check usually goes off without a hitch, whether or not maintenance issues are detected. Hotel rooms are cleaned according to the hotel company's standard. Passengers clear security checkpoints at airports around the world. And there most definitely are many, many electric bills produced.

The reason each of these processes occurs reliably, *regardless of the employee involved*, is because:

- Employees are definitely made aware of job function: the duties, tasks, and processes for which they are responsible—especially vital processes such as cash handling, safety, and other compliance-related procedures.
- There is likely documentation to support the successful execution of job function in the form of checklists, policies, processes, service models, etc.
- Employees are likely trained (sometimes extensively) to successfully execute the process.

- The proper execution of the documented process is mandatory; it's what employees are paid to do.
- There is a clear, often documented expectation of employees by management of what success looks like.
- If employees do receive feedback from their immediate supervisors, the feedback likely pertains to the proper execution of job function.
- Employees often see the proper execution of the process modeled by their immediate supervisors (regardless of the supervisor involved).

Why Extraordinary Customer Service Is Rare

Bank tellers, automotive service technicians, hotel housekeepers, TSA personnel, and a variety of other service providers may properly execute their job functions consistently, but they may or may not smile, make eye contact, add energy to their voices, or in any way reflect job essence to their customers.

The reason job essence is demonstrated inconsistently is *because of the employee involved*. If a customer encounters an employee who is engaged and genuinely interested in providing customer service, then she will likely be well served. But if she encounters an apathetic employee who is indifferent toward providing customer service, then she will likely be disappointed.

The reason employees fail to reflect job essence consistently is because:

- Employees are largely unaware of job essence.
- There is rarely documentation to support the consistent demonstration of job essence.
- Employees are seldom trained to consistently demonstrate job essence.
- The demonstration of job essence is voluntary; employees don't have to display job essence, and most don't.
- Expectations of employees by management relative to job essence are rarely documented and are usually less clear than expectations relative to job function.

- If employees do receive feedback from their immediate supervisors, the feedback is less likely to pertain to the consistent demonstration of job essence.
- Employees may or may not see the consistent demonstration of job essence by their immediate supervisors. It simply depends on the individual supervisor.

Organizations that consistently offer superior customer service understand the distinction between job function and job essence. Rather than leaving service quality to chance, these companies take steps to normalize exceptional customer service so that it is not an exception.

How to Raise Customer Service Quality from Ordinary to Extraordinary

Most managers expect employees to offer the best customer service possible, and some managers demand it. However, you cannot create extraordinary customer service by force or edict any more than you can require a customer to be delighted. But there are some concrete actions you can begin taking today that will prepare your employees to raise their quality of customer service from ordinary to extraordinary:

- Ask your employees to describe for you what their jobs entail.
- Share the key lessons and terms from this book.
- Recognize the totality of your employees' job roles.
- Raise and reinforce standards and expectations.
- Incorporate job essence into job function wherever possible.

Ask Your Employees to Describe for You What Their Jobs Entail

In Chapter 1, I said that the first thing to do to increase awareness and improve the quality of customer service delivery in any business is to ask employees this question: "Would you describe for me, from your perspective, what you do—what your job entails?"

It's likely that, if managers from a variety of businesses were to pose this question to employees, the responses received would apply exclusively to the employees' job functions. Rarely would employees reference actions or behaviors pertaining to job essence.

For example, if a health club manager asked an employee staffing the reception desk to describe what her job entails, her response presumably would include greeting members, swiping their membership cards, answering phones, registering members for classes, and accepting payments. Since everything on her list pertained to job function, this would provide the manager with an opportunity to apologize to the employee for originally explaining her job incompletely.

He could then suggest that, in addition to the job functions required of her position, her responsibilities also include making guests feel welcome, reinforcing a sense of belonging, and promoting relationships among members. All of these responsibilities pertain to job essence, which, for most health club employees, is to create promoters of the club. Health clubs succeed or fail based on the loyalty of members and members who are intent on recommending the club to others, in addition to the collection of membership dues and other revenue.

While membership cards need to get swiped and phones need to be answered, whether or not the health club thrives is ultimately determined by whether or not members feel welcome, enjoy a sense of belonging, and establish relationships with other club members. This is one reason that successful clubs stage comfortable areas for members to congregate before and after workouts and frequently sponsor social events. These clubs know that while it's easy to be lured away to a newly opened health club that is closer to home, has more amenities, or offers a lower monthly membership fee, it's more difficult to abandon the relationships formed with other club members and club personnel.

This awareness may lead to the reception desk agent sincerely complimenting a member on the commitment he has demonstrated to his exercise regimen, in addition to greeting him as she swipes his membership card. Or, instead of simply registering a member for an upcoming Pilates class, she may now share unique knowledge about the instructor such as "You're going to love Karen! She coauthored a book on Pilates exercise and really knows her stuff. Her classes are so popular that we've added two classes to the schedule."

Share the Key Lessons and Terms from this Book

Another action managers can take to raise customer service quality from ordinary to extraordinary is to share the key lessons and terms from this book. The first step in any successful behavior change is awareness. Employees don't know what they don't know.

The information below captures these lessons and terms:

- **Job function vs. job essence:** Job function refers to the duties or tasks associated with a job role. Job essence is the most critical aspect—the highest priority—of every service industry employee's job role. For most service industry employees, their highest priority at work is to create a promoter.
- **Promoter:** A promoter is a customer who is less price-sensitive, has higher repurchase rates, and is responsible for 80 to 90 percent of the positive word of mouth about a company or brand.
- **Three truths of exceptional customer service:**
    1. It reflects job essence.
    2. It is always voluntary.
    3. It typically costs no more to deliver than average service. In other words, it's free.
- **Seven simple ways to raise your customer service from ordinary to extraordinary:**
    1. Express genuine interest.
    2. Offer sincere and specific compliments.
    3. Share unique knowledge.
    4. Convey authentic enthusiasm.
    5. Use appropriate humor.
    6. Provide pleasant surprises.
    7. Deliver service heroics.

Recognize the Totality of Your Employees' Job Roles

If customer service quality is going to improve, leaders must validate the significance of job essence in the same way they currently reinforce the importance of job function. In order to accomplish this, they must consider what they currently do to promote the successful execution of job function and, where applicable, do the same for job essence. (See Figure 9-1.)

Because managers tend to focus almost exclusively on job function, most employees are aware of their responsibility to execute those aspects of their jobs and are proficient in this facet of their work. As a result:

- **There is likely a lot of structure around the job functions for which employees are responsible.** This structure takes the form of policies, procedures, protocols, checklists, and current best methods. These are almost always documented to preserve organizational memory, support new-hire training, and foster consistency.
- **Pre-shift and department meeting agendas typically are made up of topics pertaining to employees' job functions.** Energy flows where attention goes, and managers pay a lot of attention to these aspects of the job. It's natural for employees to channel their energy in the direction of their manager's focus.
- **Employees are routinely held accountable to the proper execution of job functions.** When deviation from the recognized standard operating procedure occurs, employees are made aware of the discrepancy and adjust their performance accordingly. If they are

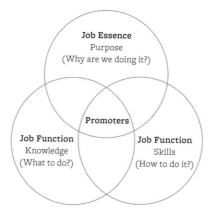

FIGURE 9-1 Three overlapping circles demonstrating job function (knowledge and skills) and job essence (purpose).

unwilling or unable to adhere to the standard, then they should be retrained, reassigned, or released by the organization.

- **It's not uncommon for these functions to be the source of contests and incentives (e.g., most loyalty program members enrolled, most bottles of wine sold, fewest mishandled baggage claims).** This also elevates the significance of the associated job functions in the minds of employees.
- **Managers often heighten awareness for the proper execution of job function by modeling desired performance.** Because managers are often promoted from within or trained in the same systems and processes used by hourly employees, most have the knowledge and skill to demonstrate the proper execution of the employee job functions they oversee.

Job essence, on the other hand, reflects employees' motivation. Employees are typically less clear about this dimension of their job roles because they are primarily focused on job function. In order for job essence to register on employees' radars, managers must:

- **Add structure to job essence.** By documenting job essence in the way that organizations naturally document job function, it's possible to realize some of the same benefits, such as preserving organizational memory, supporting new-hire training, and fostering consistency.
- **Spend a lot of time communicating the importance of job essence.** Pre-shift and department meeting agendas should include topics pertaining to employees' job essence. Managers must recognize that energy flows where attention goes. As expected, employees tend to channel their energy in the same direction as their manager's focus.
- **Hold employees accountable for the consistent demonstration of job essence.** When deviation from the recognized performance standard occurs, as with job functions, employees should be made aware of the discrepancy and adjust their performance accordingly. If they are unwilling or unable to adhere to the standard, then they should be retrained, reassigned, or released by the organization.

- **Recognize job essence by making it the source of contests and incentives (e.g., customer satisfaction, intent to return/repurchase, intent to recommend, highest client retention/renewal rates).** This also elevates the significance of job essence in the minds of employees.
- **Heighten awareness for the consistent demonstration of job essence by modeling desired behavior.** This requires that managers be intentional about practicing the behaviors outlined in this book to improve customer service quality and make lasting positive impressions on customers. Service is a verb. As such, it requires deliberate action.

Managers are largely tasked with running a profitable operation within a given budget. In order to accomplish this, they typically oversee the execution of a set of defined job functions associated with one or more job roles. This is not the problem. The problem is when managers focus solely on job functions and neglect job essence.

Many organizations unwittingly create systems or processes that undermine service quality. Perhaps the most common are call centers, where employees are evaluated based on the quantity of phone calls processed and how quickly they can end those calls. In these environments, employees are conditioned to treat calls as timed transactions rather than opportunities to serve customers.

Due to an all-too-typical myopic focus on job function in the workplace, the work routinely gets done even as customers are consistently underserved. Job essence—reflected by whether or not employees choose to express genuine interest, convey authentic enthusiasm, provide pleasant surprises, or in some other way delight customers—is often left to chance.

Managers can neutralize this uncertainty by designing systems and processes that serve customers rather than frustrate them, communicating the totality of employees' jobs by reinforcing both job function *and* job essence, and managing employees' performance through words and actions with the goal of normalizing exceptional customer service.

Raise and Reinforce Standards and Expectations

Before you can expect to raise customer service quality, you must first raise standards and expectations—unless, of course, your organization has already documented high standards for product and service quality that have been inconsistently enforced.

Exceptional customer service is never a happy accident. It is always the result of intention and design. It requires that a deliberate choice be made—for instance, the decision at Kohl's to offer a "No Questions Asked—Hassle Free" return policy for all purchases, or the choice at 1-800-PetMeds to pleasantly surprise dog owners by including a free gourmet dog biscuit with each order. Similarly, it's no accident that customers are unlikely to encounter an unresponsive phone rep at Zappos, an apathetic salesperson at Nordstrom, or a stray napkin lying along Disneyland's Main Street, U.S.A. These companies have set exceedingly high performance standards, and their employees are acutely aware of them. Employees also recognize both their job responsibilities as well as their higher purpose: to create delighted customers.

Most companies have standards in place and expectations that employees will honor them. Unfortunately, as a result of management apathy and lack of enforcement over time, these standards recede to the point where employees become apathetic, exhibiting an attitude of unconcern or indifference toward customers.

Have you ever noticed that the same employees who act indifferently toward customers snap to attention in the presence of the company's division president? Retail employees, for instance, often feel comfortable texting, smoking outdoors near store entrances, and complaining or bantering in the presence of customers, but they anxiously prepare for a planned visit by the corporate brass by waxing the floors, shining their shoes, and pressing their uniforms.

Perhaps this is because most employees rarely come into contact with the division president and thus are not familiar with him. Oh sure, they may know his name, but they are generally not familiar to the point of lowering their guard or relaxing in his presence. Not so with customers. Frontline employees come into contact with customers all the time. And whether or not they recognize a particular customer, there is a sense of familiarity with customers in general. And where there is excessive comfort and familiarity, there may be contempt—a subtle lack of respect—and a tendency to take the relationship for granted.

It's not that employees don't know what superior customer service is or how to deliver it. They do. And they consistently showcase this behavior in the presence of the division president. The issue is that many employees seem disaffected regarding customers, as if to say, "Oh, you're just a customer. For a minute there I thought you were someone important like the division president."

I just listed three behaviors that I regularly observe employees doing in retail settings: texting, smoking outdoors near store entrances, and complaining or bantering in the presence of customers. These behaviors are chronic. They occur frequently. However, when the division president is on-site, these behaviors are exceptions.

The best operations do not distinguish between a scheduled site visit by the division president and the daily opening of the store to service customers. Sure, there may be a bit of anxiety associated with the presence of a company executive—that's natural—but the company's high standards and expectations of employee performance do not wane in the absence of muckety-mucks from headquarters.

Nordstrom comes to mind as an example of a retailer that shines whether a customer or Blake Nordstrom is entering the shoe department. The last time I was in Nordstrom, an employee from the men's department walked me to the women's department in search of an umbrella for my wife. When we returned to the men's department, I also decided to buy a bottle of cologne. It was an impulse buy—in the moment. I had not planned to buy it and, in the absence of his exceptional service, I would not have.

Here is an assignment for division presidents everywhere: If they *really* want to see how their operations run, they should stop by unannounced in a baseball cap and jeans over the weekend. The goal is not to say "Gotcha!" or embarrass anyone. It's to observe and take mental notes about what they see—both assets and liabilities.

Then, assuming there is a gap (or chasm) between what they observed during their last official visit and this one, they should take action by establishing or reinforcing credible standards to guide employees' behavior. They should ensure that each manager is aware of the standards and actively uses them to manage their employees' performance. And, perhaps most important, they should hold managers accountable to model these standards at all times. If they don't, the standards are no longer credible and become unenforceable.

Although employees are responsible for their personal conduct and performance in the workplace, their employers are responsible for raising and reinforcing standards and expectations. When employees observe their immediate supervisors modeling and reinforcing these standards, they will perform similarly. As a result, employees will recognize that it is unacceptable to appear aloof or indifferent toward customers. They will no longer feel comfortable texting friends, smoking outdoors near store entrances, and complaining or bantering in the presence of customers. Instead, they will begin to treat customers with the same courtesy, respect, and sense of urgency with which they treat the division president. And their customers will notice.

Incorporate Job Essence into Job Function Whenever Possible

The most effective way for companies to ensure that employees consistently demonstrate job essence in the same way they routinely execute job functions is to incorporate the former into the latter. Although it's simple to do, it's difficult to do well.

Scripting and legislating customer greetings may appear to be an effective way to capture job essence (expressing genuine interest in the customer) in a job function (greeting customers), but that may not always be the case. When I think of ineffective greetings, I think of Papa Murphy's Take 'N' Bake Pizza. The workers at the location nearest my home practice a behavior that is intended to make customers feel welcome in their stores, but because the greeting has been scripted and mandated, its effect on customers has actually been marginalized.

Oftentimes when I enter Papa Murphy's to pick up my family's order, employees behind the counter hear the door chime and say, "Welcome to Papa Murphy's," but they don't even bother to look up from the pizzas they're assembling. As a result, this greeting is ineffective at making customers feel genuinely welcomed. This illustrates how job essence can be institutionalized (by mandating a standard greeting) as a job function. The danger, of course, is to rely on standardized practices to "wow" guests and deemphasize the spontaneity that ordinarily accompanies job essence.

This is what happened at the Ritz-Carlton after guests remarked that nearly every employee they encountered responded to requests with, "My pleasure." At first, it was fresh and unique, conveying professionalism while expressing genuine interest in serving the guest (job essence). Over time, however, it became a bit rehearsed and predictable and lost its uniqueness and charm.

Now, in order to convey more sincerity and spontaneity, the Ritz-Carlton encourages "ways of being" as opposed to "ways of doing" by suggesting that employees vary their replies to guests' requests (e.g., saying, "My pleasure," "Absolutely," "Right away," or "Certainly"), recognizing that these responses are always preferable to "No problem."

There are other companies that are effectively incorporating job essence into job function as well. For example, in Denver, there is an establishment downtown called the Broker Restaurant that provides a complimentary shrimp bowl with the purchase of two or more entrees in the same way many fine dining restaurants provide a basket of bread. While a basket of bread is typical, ordinary, routine, and expected, the shrimp bowl (for first-time guests) is unique, extraordinary, fresh, and unexpected. Placing the shrimp bowl on the diners' table is a job function, just like providing a glass of water or a basket of bread, which reflects job essence: providing a pleasant surprise.

While working in the Bahamas, I stopped by a delicatessen at the Atlantis hotel on Paradise Island to buy a roast beef sandwich. When I placed the to-go order, I mentioned to the server that I was ordering the sandwich for lunch the following day. The server confirmed the type of bread and some other specifications of my sandwich, then disappeared in the direction of the kitchen. When she returned, she handed me my order, pointing out that she had taken the time to group and individually wrap the ingredients in wax paper to keep them fresh and separate until I was ready to assemble the sandwich at lunchtime the next day.

If this was the restaurant's policy (a job function) for preparing to-go orders intended to be consumed the following day, then it illustrates how the essence of the server's job (express genuine interest, provide a pleasant surprise) could be captured in a job function. Now, I doubt this is standard policy at the delicatessen. More likely, I was fortunate to encounter a motivated server who made the choice to express genuine interest in me, anticipate my needs, and provide me with a pleasant surprise.

Last year I worked with a client, Victor Aragona, general manager of the Boston Marriott Long Wharf hotel. One observation he made was that, although his staff was friendly, there were numerous occasions when hotel associates (Marriott International's term for its employees) would huddle in small groups and banter, some with their backs to hotel guests and others with hands in their pockets. This disturbed Victor because he knew the power of first impressions. (Researchers from New York University have found that we make eleven major decisions about one another in the first seven seconds of meeting.)

At the same time, Victor recognized that associates were largely doing what they were supposed to do. Front desk agents, for example, were encouraged to come out from behind the counter to engage hotel guests in the lobby, asking them questions about their hotel stays, providing directions, and answering other questions about hotel amenities, local attractions, and restaurants. The agents were doing all these things.

Victor and his executive team became aware of the fact that every associate's job is made up of two parts: job function and job essence. They realized that associates were largely competent in their ability to execute the job functions for which they were hired. They decided that the opportunity lay with the second part of associates' job roles: the part that was trumpeted during the hiring and onboarding process but then omitted from job descriptions and management feedback (both of which tended to focus on job function). The executive team made a commitment to focus on the totality of every associate's job role, which includes both job function *and* job essence.

Associates were already well aware of their job functions: what to do and how to do it. These had been covered thoroughly in their job descriptions, throughout their on-the-job training, and were reinforced by the job-specific feedback received from their immediate supervisors. But associates were less aware of the essence of their jobs: why they were doing it. The first concrete action the leadership team took was to add an addendum to every job description highlighting the behavioral expectations of associates.

The document stated that associates' first priority was to "provide a positive experience for all guests." Obviously, properly and efficiently executing job functions would go a long way toward providing a positive experience for all guests, and associates were well versed in these tasks and duties. But reliably executing job function is insufficient, and the addendum went on to outline a series of behaviors to avoid and to display.

Associates were discouraged from huddling in small groups to banter, having their backs to hotel guests, putting their hands in their pockets, leaning, and failing to acknowledge guests when encountered throughout the hotel. Instead, associates were prompted to express genuine interest in guests by smiling, making eye contact, adding energy to their voice, using guests' names, and other guest-focused behaviors. Now that these were specified and documented as an addendum to every associate's job description, a new level of awareness and accountability emerged.

Now, associates did not just hear supervisors say, "Remember to practice assertive hospitality" (usually after thoroughly detailing operational priorities pertaining to associates' job functions) and have to figure out for themselves what "assertive hospitality" looks like. Instead, they now had a concrete reference that reinforced the behavioral expectations of them by hotel leadership.

Did it make a difference? According to Victor, "Within six months of implementing the addendums highlighting the behavioral expectations of associates, overall guest satisfaction at our hotel increased from 67.4 percent to 88 percent, and our property rose fifty positions within the company's hotel ranking by overall guest satisfaction."

• • •

It's natural, after reading a book like this one, to want to improve customer service quality in your area of responsibility. Oftentimes, that requires the cooperation of frontline employees who work closest to the customer.

A manager's initial reaction may be to change the behavior of these employees to align with the exceptional customer service behaviors outlined in this book. "If only my employees were more attuned to expressing genuine interest, sharing unique knowledge, and providing pleasant surprises. Our customer satisfaction ratings would improve," he might think.

While awareness is an important first step, it is insufficient to sustain a change in behavior. Behavioral change is complex and is affected by a number of factors that are beyond the control of an employee's manager, such as one's receptivity to feedback, readiness or eagerness to change, or level of trust with his manager or the organization itself. While managers may be able to *influence* these factors by practicing empathy, removing barriers, providing feedback, and other motivational approaches, ultimately, they cannot *determine* them. The decision of whether or not to change is made *exclusively* by the employee.

While it's difficult to change others (changing ourselves is hard enough) who are beyond your control (not your *influence*, your *control*), it's easier to change those factors that are within your control, as Victor and his executive team demonstrated by developing a concrete set of behavioral expectations as an addendum to an existing set of job descriptions. In addition to changing expectations, it's also possible for managers to change:

- Awareness
- Priorities
- Policies
- Performance standards
- Consequences
- Standard operating procedures
- Processes/service models
- Purpose statements
- Their own behavior (modeling)

As you can see, there are a lot of factors that managers can change that will influence the behavior of employees without wasting managers' time with the assumption that, if they labor long enough, they can change their employees. Concentrating their efforts on these factors is a much better use of their time and, if done well, produces sustained rapid improvement in customer service quality.

In order to implement the lessons presented in this book, raise customer service quality, and sustain a culture of extraordinary customer service, it takes leaders at all levels of the organization who can engage employees in distinguishing between job function and job essence, manage employees' performance according to this distinction, raise and reinforce standards and expectations, and be intentional about incorporating job essence into job function.

Doing so will energize employees, have an immediate positive impact on customer service quality, create promoters of the company or brand, and initiate the organization's ascension from ordinary to extraordinary!

GETTING FROM ORDINARY TO EXTRAORDINARY

- Whereas job function is executed reliably *regardless of the employee involved*, job essence is demonstrated inconsistently *because of the employee involved*.
- The goal for companies should be to normalize exceptional customer service so that it is not an exception.
- If customer service quality is going to improve, leaders must validate the significance of job essence in the same way they currently reinforce the importance of job function.
- Due to an all-too-typical myopic focus on job function, the work routinely gets done even as customers are consistently underserved.
- Before you can expect to raise customer service quality, you must first raise standards and expectations.
- Exceptional customer service is never a happy accident that a company stumbles into. It is always the result of intention and design.
- The best operations do not distinguish between a scheduled site visit by a division president and the scheduled opening of the store to service customers.

- The most effective way for companies to ensure that employees consistently demonstrate job essence in the same way they routinely execute job functions is to incorporate the former into the latter.
- While it's difficult for managers to change others who are beyond their control (not their *influence*, their *control*), it's easier to change those factors that are within their control. Some factors within their control are awareness, priorities, policies, performance standards, consequences, standard operating procedures, processes/service models, purpose statements, and one's own behavior (modeling).

Incorporating Job Essence into Job Function

In the space provided, record examples of how you can apply concepts from the chapter to raise customer service quality that you deliver or influence from ordinary to extraordinary!

ORDINARY	EXTRAORDINARY
Provide employees with job descriptions that outline the duties or tasks associated with their job roles in order to clarify their job functions.	Provide employees with addenda to their job descriptions that highlight behavioral expectations in order to clarify their purpose, their highest priority at work.

Index